JAMAICA
ALIVE!

JAMAICA
ALIVE!

Paris Permenter & John Bigley

HUNTER

HUNTER PUBLISHING, INC.
130 Campus Drive, Edison, NJ 08818
☎ 732-225-1900; 800-255-0343; fax 732-417-1744
hunterp@bellsouth.net

Ulysses Travel Publications
4176 Saint-Denis, Montréal, Québec
Canada H2W 2M5
☎ 514-843-9882 ext 2232; fax 514-843-9448

The Boundary, Wheatley Road, Garsington
Oxford, OX44 9EJ England
☎ 01865-361122; fax 01865-361133

ISBN 1-55650-822-4
© 2000 Paris Permenter & John Bigley

Maps by K. André © 2000 Hunter Publishing, Inc.

1   2   3   4

About the Authors

John Bigley and Paris Permenter fell in love with the Caribbean over a dozen years ago and have turned their extensive knowledge of the region into an occupation. As professional travel writers and photographers, the pair contribute travel articles and photographs on the US and the Caribbean to many national consumer and trade publications. The husband and wife team have also written numerous guidebooks.

Paris and John are authors of several other Hunter guidebooks: *Adventure Guide to the Cayman Islands, Adventure Guide to the Leeward Islands, The Bahamas: A Taste of the Islands, Cayman Islands Alive!* and *Jamaica: A Taste of the Island.* Currently they're at work on *Adventure Guide to Jamaica, Antigua, Barbuda, St. Kitts & Nevis Alive!* and *Nassau & The Best of The Bahamas Alive!*

Paris and John are also frequent television and radio talk show guests on the subject of travel. Both are members of the prestigious Society of American Travel Writers (SATW) and the American Society of Journalists and Authors (ASJA).

When they're not on the road, the team resides in the Texas Hill Country near Austin.

More about Paris and John's work can be found on their website: www.parisandjohn.com.

www.hunterpublishing.com

 Hunter's full range of travel guides to all corners of the globe is featured on our exciting website. You'll find guidebooks to suit every type of traveler, no matter what their budget, lifestyle, or idea of fun. Full descriptions are given for each book, along with reviewers' comments and a cover image. Books may be purchased on-line using a credit card via our secure transaction system.

Alive! guides featured include: *Nassau & The Best of The Bahamas, Aruba, Bonaire & Curaçao, Bermuda, Buenos Aires & The Best of Argentina, Venezuela, The Cayman Islands, St. Martin & St. Barts, Antigua, Barbuda, St. Kitts & Nevis, Cancún & Cozumel* and *The Virgin Islands.*

Check out our *Adventure Guides*, a series aimed at the independent traveler who enjoys outdoor activities (rafting, hiking, biking, skiing, canoeing, etc.). All books in this signature series cover places to stay and eat, sightseeing, in-town attractions, transportation and more!

Hunter's *Romantic Weekends* series offers myriad things to do for couples of all ages and lifestyles. Quaint places to stay and restaurants where the ambiance will take your breath away are included, along with fun activities that you and your partner will remember forever.

About the Alive Guides

Reliable, detailed and personally researched by knowledgeable authors, the *Alive!* series was founded by Harriet and Arnold Greenberg.

This accomplished travel-writing team also operates a renowned bookstore, **The Complete Traveller**, at 199 Madison Avenue in New York City.

We Love to Get Mail

This book has been carefully researched to bring you current, accurate information. But no place is unchanging. We welcome your comments for future editions. Please write us at: *The Alive Guides*, c/o Hunter Publishing, 130 Campus Drive, Edison, NJ 08818, or e-mail your comments to kimba@mediasoft.net.

Contents

Charts

Maps

Introduction

What are you seeking in your Caribbean get-away? Romantic resorts? Action-packed fun? Kids' activities? Hot nightlife? Great duty-free shopping?

You're in luck – one destination has all this and more. Jamaica, the third largest island in the Caribbean, spans over 4,000 square miles and is dotted with rivers, mountains, plains, forests and caves. It also has a beautiful coastline. The island offers pulsating reggae music, rich history and bountiful attractions that highlight its lush, tropical beauty. Perhaps more than any other Caribbean island except St. Lucia, Jamaica is incredibly verdant and fertile. Fruits, orchids, bromeliads, hardwoods and ferns all thrive in its rich soil, and sugar remains a major product.

Jamaica bursts forth from its borders – there's nothing shy about this destination. Birds sing at a fevered pitch, flowers grow to gigantic proportions, some dishes are hot enough to jump off the plate, and reggae is a little louder here. When you wake up in Jamaica, you know you've arrived somewhere that's definitely different.

The Major Towns & Resort Areas

Choosing a place to stay while you're in Jamaica depends on what you're seeking from the trip. The vast island is home to several distinct resort destinations as well as a bustling capital city. Resort areas lie a few hours' drive apart on roads that twist and wind beside a jagged coast and, on the eastern end alongside the Blue Mountains, with peaks that top 7,500 feet.

Within these borders there's a place for every taste. The capital city, **Kingston**, lies on the south shore, a metropolitan area that's visited primarily for business. Most vacationers head to the resort communities along the north shore. Quiet **Port Antonio**, once a hideaway for Hollywood stars, lies to the east. Heading west, the garden city of **Ocho Rios** is popular with couples.

Montego Bay, or Mo Bay, is the first taste most visitors have of the island as it's home to the north shore airport. To the far west, **Negril** was once a hippie haven, but today it's the preferred vacation spot of both aging yuppies and free-spirited travelers who enjoy its laid-back atmosphere and unbeatable sunset views.

Montego Bay

Several "great houses," which once oversaw huge sugar plantations, are today notable visitor attractions. **Rose Hall** is one of the best-known and is an easy afternoon visit for Montego Bay guests.

The White Witch

Rose Hall was once the home of the notorious Annie Palmer, better known as the White Witch. According to legend, Annie murdered several of her husbands and slave lovers.

Nature lovers will also find plenty of fun off the beaten path. Bird spotters should make a stop at the **Rocklands Bird Sanctuary** in the village of Anchovy. This is the home of octogenarian Lisa Salmon, Jamaica's best-known amateur ornithologist. Her home is a veritable bird sanctuary filled with grassquits, saffron finches and, most especially, hummingbirds. Salmon and her guides hand-feed the birds, even the tiny hummers. Visitors can come by during the afternoons (3:30-5 pm), have a seat on the patio, and take part in this unique activity.

Ocho Rios

Ocho Rios, commonly referred to as the "garden center" of Jamaica, is remarkably fertile and lush. Flowering hibiscus, bird of paradise, bougainvillea and other tropical blooms fill the air with sweet perfume year-round. The city is also home to one of Jamaica's most recognized attractions: **Dunn's River Falls**. This spectacular waterfall is actually a series of falls that cascade from the mountains to the sea. Led by a sure-footed Jamaican guide (who wears everyone's cameras slung around his neck), groups work their way up the falls hand-in-hand, forming a human daisy chain.

Runaway Bay

The smallest resort area in Jamaica is located between Montego Bay and Ocho Rios. Several resorts draw travelers to this stretch of beach that offers easy day trips to either of the big cities.

Negril

Negril is a favorite with sunseekers, honeymooners and watersports enthusiasts. Since its early days as a haven for hippies in the 1970s, Negril has harbored an image as a wild destination. Nudity is common on the beaches of Bloody Bay, home of Hedonism II, a unique resort. Reggae clubs bring some of the island's best music to the cliffs that overlook spectacular sunsets. And you can still buy marijuana and hallucinogenic teas.

The real wildness of Negril lies outside the city limits in an area known as the **Great Morass**. Crocodiles bask in the steamy afternoon sun. Peddlers sell shrimp caught using techniques over 400 years old. Spectacular birds fill the sky with bright colors and a cacophony of exotic sounds.

Today, Negril is home of all types of resorts that attract everyone from swingers to families. The city is perhaps best known for its seven miles of beach, which offers a plethora of accommodations and plenty of small restaurants.

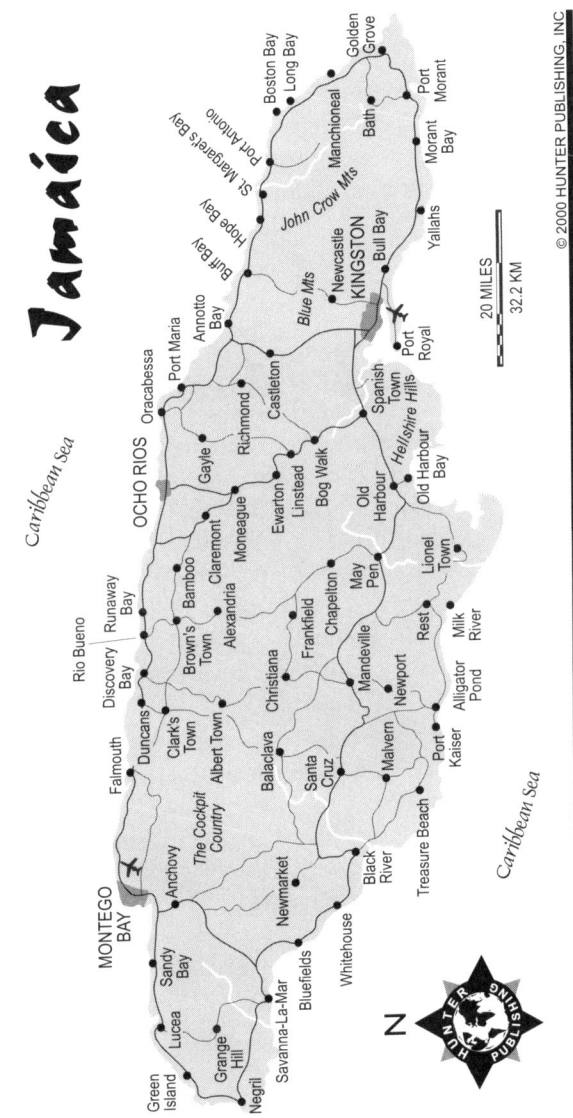

Jamaica

Caribbean Sea

Negril ✱ 5

Introduction

© 2000 HUNTER PUBLISHING, INC

MONTEGO BAY

Green Island
Lucea
Sandy Bay
Grange Hill
Negril
Savanna-La-Mar
Bluefields
Whitehouse
Anchovy
Newmarket
Black River
Treasure Beach
Port Kaiser
Alligator Pond
Milk River
Rest
Balaclava
Santa Cruz
Malvern
Newport
Mandeville
Christiana
Albert Town
Clark's Town
Duncans
Falmouth
Discovery Bay
Rio Bueno
Runaway Bay
Brown's Town
Alexandria
Frankfield
Chapelton
May Pen
Lionel Town
Bamboo
Claremont
Moneague
Linstead
Ewarton
Bog Walk
Old Harbour
Old Harbour Bay
Gayle
Richmond
Castleton
Spanish Town
Hellshire Hills
Port Royal
KINGSTON
Bull Bay
Yallahs
Newcastle
Blue Mts
Buff Bay
Hope Bay
St. Margaret's Bay
Port Antonio
Boston Bay
Long Bay
John Crow Mts
Manchioneal
Bath
Port Morant
Morant Bay
Golden Grove

The Cockpit Country

OCHO RIOS

Oracabessa
Port Maria
Annotto Bay

Caribbean Sea

20 MILES
32.2 KM

N

South Coast

Once the getaway for wealthy Kingstonians look-ing for relief from the heat, today Mandeville boasts the highest standard of living on the is-land. Perched over 2,500 feet above sea level, the community enjoys a proper English atmosphere, cool nights and is home to the Caribbean's first golf course.

Kingston

If you want to get to know the real Jamaica, you've got to spend time in Kingston.

Kingston is one Jamaica destination that's usu-ally overlooked even by long-time Jamaica travel-ers. It's easy to see why. The city is plagued by a very high crime rate and the downtown area is avoided by anyone who doesn't absolutely need to be there. However, Kingston is the heart of the is-land's cultural community, and a must-see for those interested in art, theater and dance.

Port Antonio

If you're looking for a quiet, secluded getaway, Port Antonio is the place. This lush region of Ja-maica is peaceful and unspoiled. It was once a fa-vorite with celebrity jet-setters, and today is especially popular with ecotourists and anyone who really wants to get away from it all.

The top activity in Port Antonio is a romantic raft ride aboard a bamboo float powered by a pole-maneuvering captain. If at all possible, take the two- to three-hour excursion down the **Rio**

Grande. Nearby, **Boston Beach** is known across the island for its jerk, slow-cooked in pits.

Travelers can cool off with a dip in the **Blue Lagoon**. The beautiful swimming hole that's been termed "bottomless" because of its uncanny blue hue is actually about 180 feet deep.

The Attractions

Jamaica draws vacationers to its shores again and again, with some of the island's resorts boasting the highest return clientele in the Caribbean. The secrets of this island?

- ⑤ Great weather
- ⑤ Easy access
- ⑤ Luxurious accommodations
- ⑤ Beautiful beaches
- ⑤ Lush tropical foliage
- ⑤ Fine dining
- ⑤ A variety of experiences, from rustic to ultra-elegant
- ⑤ Rich history
- ⑤ A vibrant music scene

So which area do you visit? As the Caribbean's third largest, this island spans such a huge area that you'll find very different vacation experiences in different regions. If you're looking for a laid-back, sybaritic getaway with days spent lounging under a coconut palm and nights spent dancing to reggae, Negril is for you. If you want a romantic getaway with verdant greenery, consider Ocho Rios or Port Antonio. Looking to learn more about the history and culture of the island? Kingston is for you. Have just a few days to get away so you want to make the most of every moment? Head to Montego Bay.

Golf Galore

Jamaica is home to some of the top golf courses in the Caribbean. The best-known course, and the home of the PGA's World Championship, is the **Tryall Golf Club** in Montego Bay. Other top courses include **Half Moon, Wyndham Rose Hall** and **Ironshore Golf and Country Club** in Montego Bay, **Runaway Bay** and **Sandals Golf and Country Club** in Ocho Rios, and **Negril Hills Golf Club**, just southeast of downtown Negril.

Don't be surprised to see caddies carrying the golf bags on their heads in true Jamaican style!

Day-Tripping

Whatever your destination, you're never restricted to just that one resort area. If you've got five or six days on island, take some day trips to visit more of the island's offerings. From Montego Bay, you can take a day trip to either Ocho Rios or Negril. From Ocho Rios, head down to Port Antonio for a quiet getaway. From Kingston, steal off into the lush Blue Mountains for some of the most beautiful scenery in the Caribbean. In Negril, sneak off to the South Coast for a taste of the quiet side of Jamaica.

Places to Stay & Eat

Accommodations

Prices change as quickly as the sand shifts on a Caribbean beach, so for that reason we've stayed away from providing dollar and cents figures. Besides the constantly changing prices, accommodations offer a wide variety of steps in their price scale as well: partial ocean view, full ocean view, oceanside, garden view, the list goes on and on. Each has its own price based on the month and the day of the week.

🌀 TIP

When you make your reservation, check all the available room categories to find the one that best meets your needs.

The Alive Price Scale

For accommodations, our price scale is designed to give you a ballpark figure for a typical stay during peak season. We've based these estimates on high season (December 15-April 15) for a standard room for two persons. These prices do not take into account options, such as meal plans, dive packages, etc.

Accommodations Price Scale

Prices are given in US dollars.

Deluxe......................$300+
Expensive ....$200-$300
Moderate................$100-$200
Inexpensive.............Under $100

While in Jamaica, be sure to conserve water – it's a precious commodity on the island.

All our hotel selections take major credit cards, are air-conditioned and have private baths (except in the case of the few guest houses, which are noted).

Dining

Jamaican cuisine is one of the most flavorful in the Caribbean. Spicy dishes trace their origin back to the earliest days of the island when the Arawak Indians first barbecued meats. Later, Africans, who came to the island as slaves in the days of Spanish rule, seasoned the food. In the 17th century, English influences developed the Jamaican pattie, a turnover filled with spicy meat that's a favorite lunch snack with locals. A century later, Chinese and East Indian influences made their way to Jamaica when indentured laborers, who replaced slaves after emancipation, brought their own culinary talents. Today, curried dishes grace nearly every Jamaican menu, using local meats such as goat, chicken and seafood.

Traditional Dishes

For breakfast, the national dish is **ackee and saltfish**. Ackee is a small fruit that is harvested only when it bursts and reveals its black seeds; before that time the fruit is poisonous. Ackee is cooked and resembles (and tastes much like) scrambled eggs.

The most popular dish in Jamaica is **jerk**. The meat – pork, chicken or fish – is marinated with a fiery mixture of spices, including pimento or all-spice, nutmeg, escallion, thyme and Scotch bonnet, a pepper that makes a jalapeño taste like a marshmallow. It's all served up with even more hot sauce, rice and peas, and a wonderful bread called **festival**, similar to hush puppies.

Favorite Jamaican dishes include:

Conch is a popular dish. To sound like a local, pronounce conch as KonK.

- ◎ **Ackee and Saltfish.** The national breakfast dish. You won't find ackee for sale in the United States because the fruit is poisonous when unripe.

- ◎ **Bammy.** This fried bread is made from cassava flour and is served with fried fish.

- ◎ **Curried Goat.** Chopped and highly seasoned, this dish is usually accompanied with peas and rice.

- ◎ **Duckanoo.** This delicious dessert, originally from Africa, is concocted with cornmeal, coconut, spices and brown sugar. The ingredients are tied up in a banana leaf (hence its other

names, Blue Drawers and Tie-A-Leaf),
tied, and slowly cooked in boiling water.

⊚ **Escovitch.** Escovitch is a style of cooking using vinegar, onions and spices
brought to Jamaica by the Spanish
Jews. In Jamaican grocery stores you
can find bottled escovitch sauce, which
makes preparation easy.

⊚ **Festival.** This bread is frequently
served with jerk and is similar to hush
puppies.

⊚ **Ital food.** It's not Italian food, but Ital
(eye-tal). This is the food of the Rastafarians, a vegetarian cuisine that does
not use any salt. Look for the red, green
and gold Rasta colors on dining establishments as a clue to locating Ital eateries, often small restaurants.

⊚ **Jerk.** The meat – pork, chicken or fish
– is marinated with a fiery mixture of
spices including Scotch bonnet, pimento or allspice, nutmeg, escallion
and thyme. Jerk is one of the ultimate
Jamaican dishes, dating back to the island's earliest days. The practice of
cooking the meat over the flame was
started by the Arawak Indians and
then later seasoned up by the Maroons.

⊚ **Patties.** The patty is to Jamaicans
what the hamburger is to Americans.
Ask any Jamaican and he'll tell you his
favorite patty stand. The patty is actu-

ally a fried pie, dough filled with either spicy meat or, occasionally, vegetables. One Jamaican told us his favorite was Tastee Patties, which are sold throughout the island. "They are the standard by which patties are judged," the devotee swore.

◎ **Pepperpot soup.** A savory soup made with greens and potatoes.

◎ **Fish rundown.** Fish simmered in coconut milk with breadfruit and cassava (the source of tapioca).

◎ **Rice and Peas.** Rice and red beans cooked in coconut milk.

◎ **Stamp and Go.** You could call them fast food or appetizers, but "stamp and go" seems much more descriptive. Stamp out these little fish fritters in the kitchen, grab some for the road, and go.

◎ **Breadfruit.** Similar in taste to a potato, and served in as many ways.

If you're interested to learn more about Jamaican cuisine, pick up a copy of Jamaica: A Taste of the Island.

The Alive Price Scale

For dining, we've set up a price scale based on a three-course dinner including appetizer or soup, an entrée, dessert and coffee. Cocktails and wine are extra.

Dining Price Scale

Prices are per person in US dollars.

Expensive. . . . . $40+ per person
Moderate . . . . $25-$40
Inexpensive. . . . . Under $25

A Capsule History

Jamaica has a long history, one that has shaped the island in many ways. All aspects of life, from food and music to religion, reflect the island's background.

From Indians to Europeans

The diversity and rich history of Jamaica is captivating. This island was first the home of the **Arawak Indians**, who named it Xaymaca or "land of wood and water." Those early residents came to this mountainous island around 650 A.D. and lived peacefully on the land and the sea's bounty.

★ DID YOU KNOW?

The island's coat of arms is an Arawak couple beside a shield displaying pineapples and the crest of a Jamaican alligator.

After the **Spanish** arrived in 1509, the Arawaks were soon killed or dying from disease and over-work. With the native workforce gone, the Spanish began importing African slaves, who brought with them many cooking techniques that live on to this day. Many **Spanish Jews** also arrived on the island during Spanish rule, contributing dishes such as escovitch fish, a vinegary concoction that's found on many homestyle menus.

In 1655, Spain lost Jamaica to **England**. The English turned much of the land into sugar plantations, creating many fortunes in the process.

★ DID YOU KNOW?

The term "As wealthy as a West Indian planter," became a common phrase in England, a hint at the fortunes sugar brought.

A century later, Chinese and East Indians made their way to Jamaica, replacing indentured laborers after emancipation.

The Island Today

Jamaica is an island very much in a state of change. It has undergone – and continues to experience – difficult times in the form of high unemployment, high interest rates, poverty and more. While life in the resorts is definitely easy, a quick trip outside the hotel properties will reveal a Jamaica fraught with challenges.

The People, The Culture

Jamaica's "Out of Many, One People" explains in a nutshell the rich mix of cultures that has combined to form Jamaica. Most of the residents trace their ancestry to Africa, a reminder of the island's slave days. And many other influences have come together to form the melting pot that is Jamaica.

After the abolition of slavery in 1834, workers were brought in from other countries as Jamaica looked for sources of income besides sugar. Workers from Germany, Ireland and Scotland came for a while (and one community, Seaford Town, is filled with descendants of these German settlers). Asian immigrants came from India and China and eventually workers came from what is now Lebanon.

Religion

Religion plays an important role in the lives of many Jamaicans. The island is said to have the highest number of churches per capita (surpassed only by the number of bars per capita). The Church of Jamaica, Baptist and Church of God are some of the most popular, but services are also conducted for Roman Catholics, Mormons, Jews, Hindus and others.

Rastafarianism

One of the most recognized facets of Jamaican life is the Rastafarian movement.

Rastafarians, more commonly known as Rastas, are believers in the divinity of Haile Selassie, former ruler of Ethiopia. Today, Rastas are a small sector of the Jamaican population, but because of Rastas such as the late Bob Marley, this sector is symbolic of Jamaica. Rasta men are easily identified by their dreadlocks or locks, matted waist-length strands that either flow down their back or are held beneath a knitted cap or tam. Rastafarian women generally wear locks as well, along with African clothing and headwraps.

Rastas, once discriminated against in the Jamaican society, typically band together in communities often located outside the town itself. Strong believers in the importance of natural surroundings, Rastas often live in the hills.

They are renowned herbalists, making use of folk medicine and relying on Jamaica's bounty of herbs and plants to heal many ills.

The herb for which rastafarians are best known is ganja or marijuana.

The Maroons

The Maroons are one of Jamaica's most noted groups.

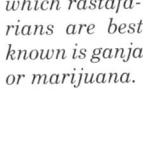

These people are descendants of the escaped slaves of the Spanish, fierce fighters who took to the hills and stayed there, never to be recaptured. They settled in a remote region south of what is now Montego Bay called **Cockpit Coun-**

try, a land of steep hills and impenetrable vegetation that is pocked with sinkholes and caves.

The name "maroon" is derived from the Spanish word "cimarron," meaning wild.

> ★ **DID YOU KNOW?**
>
> When the British took over, they called Cockpit Country the "land of look behind." Soldiers rode two to a horse, one facing front and one back, to guard against ambushes.

The Maroons, who for so long lived a self-sustained existence off the land, are still known as the island's greatest herbalists.

Today the Maroons are self-governing, with their own elected officials. The most visited community in Cockpit Country is **Accompong**, to which tours are offered. We flew over this area one time in a small four-seater traveling from Kingston to Negril and were amazed at its size, devoid of roads and marked by only a few homes. The terrain is extremely hilly and verdant, little changed from the days when the original Maroons made their homes here.

Culture & Customs

Don't be surprised if you are greeted by local residents.

The residents of Jamaica are some of the Caribbean's friendliest. Greetings are expected. Don't just walk up to a resident to ask a question – start with a friendly "good morning" or you'll be considered mannerless.

Jamaicans are known for their directness and humor. Not everyone is trying to sell you ganja or braid your hair; many people just enjoy the interaction with travelers. If you would like to meet local residents with similar interests to yours, the free **Meet the People** program is an excellent way to do so. Contact the Jamaica Tourist Board before your trip.

Service is somewhat slower in Jamaica than it is at home. Allow sufficient time at meals so you're not rushed.

Language

English is the official language of Jamaica. Standard English is spoken in all business situations and by islanders to visitors. However, locals also speak a patois, a combination of English, Spanish, Portuguese, African phrases and Jamaican slang. Spoken in a sing-song style, the patois is difficult to understand. It is not necessary for travelers to learn patois because all interactions can be accomplished in English, but you might enjoy taking a lesson. Here's an example of some patois you might hear on the streets:

Many larger hotels offer patois lessons.

a go foreign . . . . to leave Jamaica
bendung maaket . . a sidewalk market, a
             place where you would bend
             down or "bendung" to shop
boonoonunus. . . . . . wonderful, beautiful
duppy. . . . . ghost
irie (eye-ree) . . . . all's well, good
mash up. . . . . sickly, tired
nyam . . . . eat
wagga wagga. . . . . bountiful
winji. . . . . sickly

Environment

Jamaica is home to 27 endemic species of birds, including the vervain hummingbird, the second smallest in the world. The Blue Mountains are a great destination for birdwatchers and nature lovers, who can follow a series of trails through the range.

Jamaica is one of the lushest islands of the Caribbean, an amazing collection of flowering plants, fruit-bearing trees and fertile growth. The **lignum vitae** is the national flower. The flowers are produced by a tree that contains some of the world's hardest wood, used in early times to build ships. Today the blonde wood is used to make beautiful carvings.

The national tree is the **mahoe**, used to make small pieces of furniture.

The national fruit is the **ackee**, which was brought from Ghana to the island. This small, innocent-looking red fruit grows on a large evergreen tree.

⚠ WARNING

The ackee must be picked by someone knowledgeable; in its unripened state the fruit is deadly. Only when the fruit pops open to reveal black seeds is it safe to eat.

Sugarcane also grows throughout Jamaica. It is used to make the excellent rums produced on the island.

Animals & Reptiles

Although Jamaica does not have poisonous snakes, you might spot one of the island's harmless indigenous species, such as the **grass snake**. The numbers of this snake, which feeds on frogs and lizards, have been reduced by the mongoose, which was introduced to control rats.

★ DID YOU KNOW?

Unfortunately, the rat and mongoose keep different hours, so the mongoose feeds on the snake, which is the natural predator of the rat. Thus, the rat population is going strong.

On the south coast in the Black River, you'll find Jamaica's most noted reptile, the **crocodile**. These toothy beasts are protected and docile.

Birds

The **doctor bird**, the national symbol of Jamaica, is easy to spot. Just look for a hummingbird with a long streamer tail!

Another commonly seen bird is the **Zenaida dove**, a cooing dove that feeds on dried seeds. The colorful **bananaquit**, a yellow-and-black bird that's not shy about begging for crumbs (and its favorite treat, sugar) is another island resident.

Magnificent frigate birds are also sighted here. Their wings may span of over seven feet and are sharply angled like boomerangs. The black frigate bird is easy to spot. It soars high and is aggressive to other birds, often hitting the red-footed booby in flight in an attempt to make it disgorge its meal and provide an easy dinner.

Life Undersea

 For many travelers, Jamaica is a destination sought for its underwater attractions, offering excellent scuba diving, snorkeling and deep-sea fishing, along with a variety of marine life. Among the reefs, expect to see brilliant parrotfish, large-eyed squirrelfish, blue tang, stingrays, eagle rays, rock lobster and, if you're lucky, a turtle. Blue marlin, yellowfin tuna, shark and wahoo reside in the deepest waters.

⚠ WARNING

When snorkeling or diving, watch out for **fire coral**. There are many varieties, all of which are edged in white. If you accidentally brush against the coral, it will defend itself and burn you.

Climate & Weather

Jamaica enjoys a perpetual early summer climate. Days are warm year-round and almost every day is warm enough for an ocean dip, even in early morning hours. Evenings are comfortable and, during the winter months (January through March), you might even want a light sweater on some evenings.

The average temperature is 82° all year long, but it is often warmer in the afternoon, and it invariably feels much hotter because of high humidity levels. Fortunately, the island is blessed with northeasterly trade winds that keep you from sweltering.

Rainfall varies with the season. Overall, the island gets an average of 78 inches a year (one look around at the lush vegetation and you'll see it's put to good use!). The lion's share of the rain falls in the misty Blue Mountains, home of some of the world's best coffee. Usually along the coast, rain showers are brief and heavy, coming in mid-afternoon and clearing up before you can run inside.

⊙ TIP

Want to find out the weather forecast for your visit? Check out the Jamaica Tourist Board's website: www.jamaicatravel.com.

CLIMATE CHART (Kingston)		
Month	**High/Low (°F)**	**Rain days**
January	86/67	3
February	86/67	3
March	86/68	2
April	87/70	3
May	87/72	4
June	89/74	5
July	90/73	4
August	90/73	7
September	89/73	6
October	88/73	9
November	87/71	5
December	87/69	4

Rain is common in the afternoons, so plan your time at the beach accordingly.

Hurricanes

September is the worst month for hurricanes.

Mention weather and the Caribbean in the same sentence and, quite predictably, the topic of hurricanes arises. These deadly storms are officially a threat from June through November, although the greatest danger is during the later months, basically August through October.

Hurricanes are defined as revolving storms with wind speeds of 75 mph or greater. These counter-clockwise storms begin as waves off the west coast of Africa and work their way across the Atlantic, some eventually gaining strength and becoming tropical depressions (under 40 mph) or tropical storms (40-74 mph). Excellent warning systems keep islanders posted of the possibility of oncoming storms.

Getting There

By Air

International air travelers have two airport options in Jamaica: **Montego Bay** and **Kingston**. Most choose to fly into Montego Bay, which is the better option if you're heading to Montego Bay, Ocho Rios, Runaway Bay or Negril. Travelers headed to Kingston, Port Antonio and the Blue Mountains generally fly into Kingston.

A recent change in air service in the Caribbean has been the development of a hub in Montego Bay by **Air Jamaica** (☎ 800-523-6805, www.airjamaica.com). The airline was privatized in 1994 and serves as the national carrier of Jamaica, operated by Gordon "Butch" Stewart of Sandals Resorts. Air Jamaica now offers over 330 direct flights a week from Atlanta, Baltimore, Ft. Lauderdale, Los Angeles, Miami, Newark, New York (JFK), Orlando and Philadelphia to Montego Bay and Kingston. It also runs connecting service to many other island destinations, such as Barbados, Grand Cayman, Bonaire, Grenada, Havana, Nassau and St. Lucia.

Montego Bay Arrivals

Arrival in Montego Bay is at the **Donald Sangster International Airport** via the following airlines:

Air Jamaica, ☎ 800-523-5585. Service from Atlanta, Baltimore, Chicago, Ft. Lauderdale, Los Angeles, Miami, Newark, New York, Orlando, London, Manchester, Philadelphia and Toronto.

Air Jamaica Express, ☎ 876-923-8680 or 800-523-5585. Service from Santo Domingo, Grand Cayman and Belize.

Air Canada, ☎ 416-925-2311 or 800-776-3000. Service from Halifax, Montreal, Toronto and Winnipeg.

ALM, ☎ 800-327-7230 or 305-477-0955. Service from Curaçao.

American Airlines, ☎ 800-433-7300. Service from Miami and New York.

American Trans Air, ☎ 800-225-2995. Service from Indianapolis-Ft. Lauderdale (winter), Indianapolis-Orlando (summer).

British Airways, ☎ 800-247-9297 or 0181-897-4000. Service from London.

Condor, ☎ 800-542-6975. Service from Frankfurt.

Copa, ☎ 800-359-2672 or 305-477-7333. Service from Panama City, Bogota, Peru and Ecuador.

Cubana, ☎ 876-978-3406. Service from Cuba (Santiago and Havana).

LTU, ☎ 800-888-0200. Service from Dusseldorf, Germany.

Northwest Airlines, ☎ 800-225-2525. Service from Minneapolis and Tampa.

Trans World Airlines, ☎ 800-892-4141. Service from St. Louis.

USAir, ☎ 800-428-4322. Service from Philadelphia-Charlotte.

Are We There Yet?

Here's a look at flying times to Mo Bay:

```
Atlanta . . . . . . . . . . . . . . . . 2 hrs 40 mins
Baltimore . . . . . . . . . . . . . . . . . . 3 hrs
Boston . . . . . . . . . . . . . . . 3 hrs 40 mins
Charlotte . . . . . . . . . . . . . . . . . . 3 hrs
Chicago . . . . . . . . . . . . . . 3 hrs 45 mins
Cleveland . . . . . . . . . . . . . 3 hrs 15 mins
Dallas . . . . . . . . . . . . . . . 3 hrs 20 mins
Detroit . . . . . . . . . . . . . . . 3 hrs 15 mins
Ft. Lauderdale . . . . . . . . . . 1 hr 30 mins
Indianapolis . . . . . . . . . . . . . . . . 4 hrs
London . . . . . . . . . . . . . . 10 hrs 15 mins
Los Angeles . . . . . . . . . . . 5 hrs 30 mins
Miami . . . . . . . . . . . . . . . 1 hour 25 mins
Milwaukee . . . . . . . . . . . . 3 hrs 45 mins
New York . . . . . . . . . . . . . 3 hrs 20 mins
Orlando . . . . . . . . . . . . . . . . . . . 2 hrs
St. Louis . . . . . . . . . . . . . . 3 hrs 40 mins
```

Kingston Arrivals

In Kingston, the **Norman Manley International Airport** is served by:

Air Jamaica, ☎ 800-523-5585. Service from Atlanta, Chicago, Ft. Lauderdale, Miami, Newark,

New York, Orlando, London, Manchester and Toronto.

Air Jamaica Express, ☎ 876-923-8680 or 800-523-5585. Service from Santo Domingo, Grand Cayman and Belize.

Air Canada, ☎ 416-925-2311 or 800-776-3000. Service from Toronto.

ALM, ☎ 800-327-7230 or 305-477-0955. Service from Curaçao.

American Airlines, ☎ 800-433-7300. Service from New York and Miami.

British Airways, ☎ 800-247-9297 (US) or 0181-897-4000 (London). Service from London.

BWIA, ☎ 800-327-7401. Service from Antigua, Barbados, Port of Spain, St. Maarten and St. Lucia.

Cayman Airways, ☎ 800-422-9626. Service from Grand Cayman.

Copa, ☎ 800-359-2672 or 305-477-7333. Service from Panama City, Bogota, Peru and Ecuador.

By Cruise Ship

Most cruise ships arrive in **Ocho Rios** or **Montego Bay**. Both city's terminals are within easy distance of the craft markets and shopping centers.

CRUISE LINES CALLING ON JAMAICA	
Carnival Cruise Line	☎ 800-327-9501
Celebrity-Fantasy	☎ 800-437-3111
Commodore Cruise Line	☎ 800-237-5361
Costa Cruise Line	☎ 800-462-6782
Crown Cruise Line (Cunard)	☎ 800-528-6273
Dolphin Cruise Line	☎ 800-325-4763
Holland America	☎ 800-426-0327
Princess Cruises	☎ 800-421-0522
Royal Caribbean Cruise Line	☎ 800-327-6700

Introduction

Intra-Island Travel

Unlike many Caribbean islands, Jamaica is large enough to need intra-island service, which enables easy travel to and from Montego Bay, Negril, Ocho Rios, Port Antonio and Kingston (to Tinson Pen Aerodrome). The flights save time and also provide travelers with great views of the island.

We recently flew out from Kingston's Tinson Pen airport to Negril and had a view of the island like we've never seen before!

For information on these short flights, contact one of the following airlines.

INTRA-ISLAND AIR SERVICE	
Air Jamaica Express	☎ 876-923-8680 or 800-523-5585
Timair Ltd.	☎ 876-952-2516
Tropical Airlines	☎ 876-940-5917

Getting Ready

When to Visit

The peak (read: most expensive) time to visit Jamaica is mid-December through mid-April. This is the busiest time of year, a season when Americans and Canadians are looking for a warm weather refuge, if only for a few days, and when hotels and condominiums can charge peak prices. Shoulder seasons – the fall and springtime – are also excellent times to visit. Prices are lower, crowds are lighter, and the weather is generally beautiful.

Entry Requirements

US and Canadian citizens may enter Jamaica with a passport or other proof of citizenship, such as an original birth certificate with a raised seal, a naturalization certificate or a certificate of citizenship along with a photo ID (all documents must bear the same name). You'll also need to show a return or ongoing ticket.

◎ TIP

A voter registration card is no longer valid proof of citizenship!

Citizens of the **United Kingdom, Japan, Australia, Germany, Ireland** and **France** will need a valid passport and a return or onward ticket.

Customs Regulations

US Customs

US visitors can return home after a 48-hour visit with up to $600 of duty-free purchases. If you buy Jamaican art, rum, perfume, coffee or other locally made items, they are also duty-free. Visitors can mail to the US an unlimited number of gifts worth up to $100 without duty (cigars, liquors and perfumes are not included).

🌀 TIP

Before your trip, get a copy of *Know Before You Go* brochure (Publication 512) from the US Customs Service at your airport or by writing the US Customs Service, PO Box 7407, Washington, DC 20044.

Canadian Customs

With a seven-day absence from Canada, visitors may claim a $500 exemption yearly, not including alcohol and tobacco. Exemptions cannot be pooled with other travelers in your party.

British Customs

UK travelers have the following exemption: 200 cigarettes, 50 cigars or one liter of spirits for visitors age 17 or over and all other goods up to £36 value.

Japanese Customs

Japanese travelers have an exemption of up to Yen 200,000 and three bottles of liquor for travelers age 20 and over.

What to Pack

Jamaica is a casual destination for the most part. You'll feel right at home in shorts and t-shirts for the day, bathing suits and coverups for the beach, and casually elegant clothing for evening wear (dressy shorts or sundress for women, long pants and collared shirts for guys). We do recommend a few items for all visitors:

A few restaurants require jackets; we've made a note of these throughout the text.

- ❏ *Proof of citizenship*
- ❏ *Airline tickets*
- ❏ *Snorkel, fins and mask*
- ❏ *Sunscreen*
- ❏ *Aloe vera gel*
- ❏ *First aid kit*
- ❏ *Cameras, flash and film (we recommend that you bring an inexpensive underwater camera too)*
- ❏ *Drivers license for car rental*

- *Swimsuit (bring two swimsuits; high humidity means long drying times)*
- *All prescriptions (in original bottles)*
- *Address book*

> ◎ **TIP**
>
> If you'll be scuba diving, don't forget your "C" card, as well as any gear you typically bring along such as a compass, dive tables, dive computer, weight belt, mesh bag, dive boots, logbook and proof of insurance.

If you're thinking about going on a boat excursion, be sure to bring some non-skid shoes.

Sources of Information

A good place to start is the **Jamaica Tourist Board**, ☎ 800-JAMAICA, www.jamaicatravel.com. You may also contact your nearest Jamaica Tourist Board office to request free brochures and maps.

Jamaica Tourist Board Offices

In the US

Jamaica Tourist Board
801 2nd Ave., 20th floor
New York, NY 10017
☎ 212-856-9727 or 800-233-4582
500 N. Michigan Ave., Suite 1030
Chicago, IL 60611
☎ 312-527-1296

1320 S. Dixie Hwy., Suite 1101
Coral Gables, FL 33146
☎ 305-665-0557

3440 Wilshire Blvd., Suite 1207
Los Angeles, CA 90010
☎ 213-384-1123

In Canada

1 Eglinton Ave. E, Suite 616
Toronto, Ontario M4P 3A1
☎ 416-482-7850

In the UK

Jamaica Tourist Board
1-2 Prince Consort Rd.
London SW7 2BZ
☎ 0171-224-0505

In Asia

Jamaica Tourist Board
#3 Mori Building
1-4-10 Nishi-Shinbashi
Minato-ku, Tokyo 105
Japan
☎ 81-3-3591-3841, fax 81-3-3591-3845

In Germany

Jamaica Tourist Board
Postfach 90 04 37
60444 Frankfurt
☎ 49-6184-99-00-44, fax 49-6184-99-00-46

In France

Jamaica Tourist Board
32 Rue de Ponthieu
75008 Paris
☎ 33-1-45-63-4201, fax 33-1-42-25-6640

In Italy

Jamaica Tourist Board
Piazza dei Cenci 7-A
00186 Rome
☎ 39-6-687-5693, fax 39-6-687-3644

Help On-Island

You'll find visitor help stations all over the island. Drop in the office for directions, recommendations, or just to say hello.

In Kingston

Kingston has two JTB offices: a desk in the immigration entry area at Norman Manley International Airport and a main office at 2 St. Lucia Avenue in New Kingston, ☎ 876-929-9200.

In Montego Bay

Montego Bay also has two JTB locations: a desk in the immigration area at Donald Sangster International Airport and another at Cornwall Beach, ☎ 876-952-4425.

In Black River

The JTB office is located in the Hendriks Building at 2 High Street, ☎ 876-965-2074.

One of the best sources of Jamaica info is the official Jamaica Tourist Board's website: www.jamaica-travel.com.

*Have a quick question while you're on island? Call the **JTB helpline** from anywhere on the island at ☎ 1-888-995-9999.*

In Negril

You'll find the JTB office on the second floor of the Coral Seas Plaza, ☎ 876-957-4243.

In Ocho Ríos

A JTB office is on the second floor of the Ocean Village Shopping Centre (right above the grocery store), ☎ 876-974-2570.

In Port Antonio

The office is in the City Centre Plaza, ☎ 876-993-3051.

Once You Arrive

Crime

Crime is a serious problem in Jamaica. Use the same precautions you'd exercise at home and then some.

- ⊚ Don't leave money on the beach while you swim.
- ⊚ Don't leave cash and valuables in your hotel room; use your hotel safe.
- ⊚ Don't go out for walks on lonely stretches of beach or on quiet roads after dark.

Crime is particularly a problem in Kingston, as in any metropolitan area. Use big city precautions and heed advice to stay away from downtown, especially after dark. We've pointed out particularly dangerous areas to avoid in the Kingston chapter. It's also a good idea to check with your hotel concierge for safety suggestions in Kingston.

You may very well be familiar with Jamaica's latest problem due to news headlines. In April 1999 Jamaica experienced a brief slowdown in tourism due to riots over an increase in the gasoline tax. There were some deaths in Kingston and some tourists were unable to make their flights due to blocked roads. However, business has quickly returned to normal, although tourism numbers did fall. "The fallout caused by the demonstrations has had an adverse effect on the industry," said Francis Tulloch, Minister of Tourism.

Jamaica continues to focus its attention on visitor safety. "We are being honest with issues of safety," said Jamaica Tourist Board chairman Adrian Robinson. "We take tourism extremely seriously. We are focusing our government's attention on this." Incidents against tourists have been on the decrease, falling from 380 incidents against one million tourists in 1989 to 280 incidents against 1.2 million tourists in 1998.

Drugs

Marijuana, or ganja as it's known locally, is illegal throughout Jamaica. Drug penalties are becoming stiffer, and drug prevention measures more stringent in many countries. Customs carefully screens bags of passengers both leaving the island

and entering the US mainland (using dogs in most cases).

The come-ons to tourists vary from vendor to vendor, but expect to be approached by friendly young men who introduce themselves by name, shake your hand, and ask "is this your first time to Jamaica?" Other approaches include, "Remember me from yesterday?" and "I met your friend down the beach." From there the offers extend from motorcycles rides to see fields of ganja to attempts at selling "party stuff" or "stuff I grew myself."

Young travelers (especially males) are prime targets for ganja salesmen.

As is the case with market and beach vendors, dealing with drug entrepreneurs also just requires firm politeness. "No, thank you," will generally end the transaction. Stay cool, move on, and realize that these businessmen are just out to make a buck, which on this island is not always an easy proposition.

⚠ WARNING

We caution vacationers not to return home with packages that they have not personally packed. We have been approached by locals asking us to mail packages for them once we arrived in the US. The requests may have been legitimate, but the risk is too great.

Electrical Current

Throughout the island, you'll find 110 volts, 50 cycles. Standard American plugs are used. American and Canadian appliances can be used, but you might find that they run a little hot.

A few hotels run on 220 volts. Be sure to ask when you make your hotel booking.

> ## 🌀 TIP
>
> Need a converter? Check your hotel's front desk for a loan.

Money Matters

Cash

Do not plan to use your ATM card in Jamaica. Machines accept only Jamaican bank cards. ATM cash advances can be made on some credit cards if you have a PIN number. Without your PIN, you'll need to visit the bank clerk. Note, however, that this can be a slow proposition. We ran out of cash in Negril recently and spent close to two hours obtaining a cash advance from the local bank. There are better ways to spend your holiday.

See the currency conversion chart on page 99.

See the currency conversion chart on page 99.

Cash, cash, cash!

We cannot recommend strongly enough that you bring enough cash for your trip. Without ATMs as an option, it's easy to find yourself stranded. Make it easy on yourself and just bring cash and/or travelers' checks. You'll need cash for market purchases, taxi rides, and the departure tax (presently US$27 per person).

Banking

Banks are open 9 am-2 pm, Monday to Thursday; 9 am-12 pm and 2:30-5 pm on Friday. We have included a list of banks following each city section.

Tipping

Tips are generally not expected for short taxi rides.

A service charge is added to the bill at most restaurants. If that's not the case, a 10-15% tip is customary. Remember that tips are part of the package at many all-inclusive resorts; check with yours.

Tip Guideline

- ◎ Restaurants: 15% of bill, but check first to see if a service charge has already been included.

- ◎ Bars: US $1 per drink.

- ◎ Airport skycap-porter: US 50¢ per bag.

◎ Taxis: 10-15% for longer rides, but not expected for short ones.

◎ Hotel bell desk: US$1 per bag or to call a cab.

◎ Hotel housekeeping: US$1 per person, per day at non-all-inclusives.

◎ Hotel room service: 15% of bill at non-all-inclusives.

◎ Parking attendant-valet: US$1-2.

◎ Haircare-personal services: 15% of bill.

Newspapers-Broadcast Media

The largest island newspaper is Kingston's *The Jamaica Gleaner*, a daily. The paper is distributed at grocery stores around the island; you can also see selected stories on-line (www.jamaica-gleaner.com). *The Jamaica Observer* is published daily and serves as the afternoon paper.

Radio stations include **HOT 102 FM**, **Irie FM** (105.1, 105.5, 107.1, 107.3, 107.7), **KLAS FM** (89.5, 89.1, 89.9), **POWER 106 FM**, **FAME FM** (95.7, 92.7, 91.5, 98.1, 95.7, 95.3, 95.9) and **Radio Jamaica** (94.5, 94.1; AM 550, AM 720).

Two television stations serve the island: **CVM Television** (channel 4 in Kingston, channel 11 in Montego Bay) and **JBC** (channels 7 and 11 in Kingston, channel 10 in Montego Bay).

Telephones

As much as we love Jamaica, we must admit that this island is one of the worst places in the Caribbean from which to make a telephone call. The reason? Most American telephone companies will not accept credit card calls from Jamaica due to the high volume of fraudulant credit card use. But there are solutions.

- ◎ Dial direct from your hotel. This is the most expensive solution. If you do this, call home and have the recipient call you right back, as calls made from the mainland to Jamaica are far less expensive. Hotel markups on your outgoing call are hefty.

- ◎ Call home collect. This is less expensive than a direct call, but pricier than our next option.

- ◎ Buy a Jamaican phone card *on the island*. They are sold at local grocery stores and come in various denominations. A J$200 card buys about three minutes worth of talk time to the US.

◎ TIP

We once bought an "international" calling card in Miami that wouldn't work in Jamaica. Wait until you arrive on the island to purchase the card.

Introduction

⊚ Fax service is available at just about all the resorts and is another good way to keep in touch. Many charge nothing to receive a fax and only a few dollars to transmit.

Within Jamaica, there are two telephone charges: J15¢ per minute for calls within the parish and J76¢ per minute (or J38¢ during off peak times) for calls from one parish to another

Time Zone

Eastern Standard Time is observed year-round. Jamaica does not observe Daylight Savings Time.

Holidays & Festivals

January 1 . . . . New Year's Day
February-March . . . . . . Ash Wednesday
March or April . . . . Good Friday&
                            Easter Monday
May 23 . . . . Labour Day
August (1st Mon.) . . . Independence Day
October (3rd Mon.) National Heroes Day
December 25 . . . . Christmas Day
December 26 . . . . Boxing Day

Annual Celebrations

The Jamaica Tourist Board offers information, including dates, for all of the events listed here. Call them at ☎ 800-JAMAICA.

☼ January

Accompong Maroon Festival, *St. Elizabeth*

This early-January festival celebrates the Maroon culture in the parish of St. Elizabeth in western Jamaica. Festivities, which date back to the 19th century, include feasts, blowing of the Abeng (a wind instrument), and playing of the Maroon drums. This unique festival is little attended by travelers, but is a good event if you're looking to get off the beaten path.

☼ February

Bob Marley Week with Reggae Sunsplash, *Kingston and Ocho Rios*

The memory of reggae great Bob Marley is remembered with a week of activities, including art exhibits, seminars at the Bob Marley Museum and, finally, concerts at Reggae Sunsplash in Ocho Rios' White River Reggae Park. This is a must for true Marley lovers. Early February.

Sugar Cane Ball, *Montego Bay*

One of the most elegant events of the year is the Sugar Cane Ball, held in February at Round Hill Hotel in Montego Bay. For over two decades, this formal ball has raised money for local charities. Visitors can buy tickets.

☼ March

Negril Music Festival, *Negril*

This three-night festival showcases the talents of local reggae and calypso singers as well as international performers. Mid-March.

☼ April

Devon House Easter Craft Fair, *Kingston*

Shop for locally produced arts and crafts and enjoy traditional food and drink at this annual event. Like the Christmas Crafts Festival, this event is held at historic Devon House.

Carnival, *Ocho Rios, Kingston and Montego Bay*

In April, Ocho Rios, Montego Bay and Kingston celebrate Carnival. The week-long event includes street parades, fetes, and a general feeling of celebration. Visitors can join in the fun.

Red Stripe Horse Show & Gymkhana, *Ocho Rios*

Horse lovers can enjoy the Red Stripe Horse Show and Gymkhana at Chukka Cove in Ocho Rios, an annual event that brings in top riders from Jamaica, Europe and the US.

☼ June

Ocho Rios Jazz Festival, *Ocho Rios*

Summer brings plenty of music to the island, starting with this festival, which offers a week of international performers from the US, England, France, Holland, Japan and the Caribbean. Jazz events take place in Ocho Rios as well as Montego Bay, with jazz teas, jazz festivals on the river, jazz barbecues and more.

☀ July

Jamaica Spice, Ocho Rios

This special event is a treat for those with an interest in Jamaican food. For two days, the park adjacent to Renaissance Jamaica Grande fills with arts, crafts, music and literature, all tied together under the theme of food. Traditional Jamaican dishes – jerk pork, escovitch fish, fish and bammy, ackee and saltfish, coconut drops – is served. Locally made products such as coffee candles, edible flowers, sauces and seasonings are for sale. Cooking demonstrations on "the secret of jerking" draw crowds; other events include a professional culinary competition, a gala diner, and a cookbook signing by Jamaican culinary writers. Traditional dances, musical performances, donkey rides, face painting for kids and art displays round out the weekend of fun.

To learn more about Jamaican cuisines, pick up a copy of our other book, *Jamaica, A Taste of the Island*. It features travel information as well as island recipes and cooking tips from the island's best chefs.

Negril Carnival, Negril

Join in the fun with parades, concerts, mento band competitions and more. Late July and early August. This carnival is on a smaller scale than the blow-out in Kingston, but it's still great fun.

☼ August

Jamaica Independence Day Parade, *Kingston*

This parade features uniformed groups and bands. Held on August 6th each year to celebrate the country's independence from Britain, which was granted in 1962.

Montego Bay Yacht Club Marlin Tournament, *Montego Bay*

For nearly four decades this event has drawn participants from around the island as well as from other regions. Call the yacht club at ☎ 876-979-8038 for information about participating in this five-day event.

Reggae Sumfest, *Montego Bay*

One of the largest musical events on the island. This extravaganza draws local and international talent. Sumfest is one of the top music events in the Caribbean!

☼ September

Air Jamaica Jazz and Blues Festival, *Ocho Rios*

This month-long event brings in both local talent and internationally recognized names. A must for music buffs!

☼ October

Terra Nova's Heritage Food Festival, *Kingston*

Jamaica's culinary heritage is the focus of this week. Regional dishes complemented by local music. The festival spans a full week; all events take place at the elegant Nova Hotel.

☼ November

Harmony Hall's Anniversary Show, *Ocho Rios*

The elegant Harmony Hall exhibits the works of local artists during this annual show from mid-November through early December.

Caribbean Heritage Festival, *St. Catherine*

Want to learn more about the music and food of the Caribbean? Here is your chance. Now in its fourth year, this three-day festival showcases the heritage of the many different cultures found in the Caribbean.

☼ December

Devon House Christmas Fair, *Kingston*

Shop for Jamaican art, crafts and local foods at this annual event. The three-day shopping extravaganza is held at the historic Devon House.

Weddings

Getting married in Jamaica is easy and inexpensive, with just a 24-hour waiting period after you arrive on the island. No blood tests are required. Most larger resorts have excellent wedding consultants on staff who can handle all the arrangements, from license to flowers. Contact your resort beforehand to get the paperwork rolling. You'll probably need to fax or courier copies of your documents to the resort, but be sure to bring along the original copy on your trip!

You'll need to supply the following:

◎ **Proof of citizenship.** Bring along a certified copy of your birth certificate (one with a raised seal), which includes your father's name.

◎ **Parent's written consent**, if one of you is under 21.

◎ **Proof of divorce** (if applicable). Either a certified copy or original Certificate of Divorce is required.

◎ Copy of **Death Certificate** for widow or widower.

The SuperClubs resorts offer free weddings! Call ☎ 800-GO-SUPER for details.

Montego Bay

Introduction

For many tourists, Jamaica is synonymous with Montego Bay. This north coast community is the capital of the Jamaica's tourism industry. Most visitors arrive by air, but this is also a popular cruise ship destination.

As home of the north shore Airport, Montego Bay, or Mo Bay, is the first taste most visitors have of the island. It is the second largest city on the island and has the busiest cruise pier. Travelers from around the world come and go in this bustling community year-round.

★ DID YOU KNOW?

The name Montego is derived from "manteca," or lard in Spanish. The Spanish first named this "Bahia de Manteca" or Lard Bay. Why? The Spanish once shipped hogs from this port city.

Columbus chose to christen the site with a more dignified moniker: El Golfo de Buen Tiempo, which means Bay of Good Weather.

In 1924 Jamaican tourism got its start right here in Mo Bay and there has been no looking back.

The Mo Bay Tourist

While Montego Bay suits many vacationers, there are definitely some who will enjoy it more than others. The following travelers might consider a stay here:

- ◎ Visitors with a **limited stay**. Many resorts here are just minutes from the airport so those with three- and four-night stays would do well to choose Mo Bay over other resort areas such as Negril and Ocho Rios, almost a two-hour drive away.

- ◎ **Scuba divers**. Montego Bay is considered one of the top scuba areas on the island.

- ◎ **Families**. Montego Bay is home to several excellent family resorts, such as Wyndham Rose Hall.

- ◎ **Shoppers**. The city is the top shopping area on the island.

- ◎ **Golfers**. Many of the top golf courses are located in the Montego Bay area.

- ◎ **First-time visitors**. If it's your first time to Jamaica, Montego Bay is an excellent choice. From here you can take day trips in several directions to sample other areas of the island or just enjoy the city's delightful attractions.

THREE-DAY MONTEGO BAY ITINERARY	
Day One	Arrive Mo Bay. Check in at your hotel, then hit the beach. Check with tour desk about possible tours on future days (some tours are only offered a few times a week). Schedule any spa treatments, scuba times, tee times, or lessons for your stay. Enjoy a relaxing dinner.
Day Two	Enjoy the beach, golf or watersports in the morning. Shop in the afternoon in Mo Bay's duty-free shops or the crafts market. Visit the "Hip Strip" for dinner and nightlife.
Day Three	Enjoy the beach, golf or watersports in the morning. Take a tour of Rose Hall and hear about the White Witch of Jamaica. Order a traditional Jamaican meal followed by a reggae show.

Montego Bay

Arrival

Getting to Montego Bay is simple; the city's Donald Sangster International Airport is the nation's busiest. You'll find air service directly into Montego Bay from numerous carriers (see the *Introduction* for a complete listing).

Getting To Your Hotel

Once you arrive at the airport, proceed to Immigration. You'll be given a Jamaican Immigration card on the plane or at your departing airport.

> **⊚ TIP**
>
> These lines can be long, so it pays to have your completed immigration card (use blue or black ink only).

A passport will help push you through the process fastest.

Head to the "Visitors" line and move on through immigration. Have your proof of citizenship (either passport or certified birth certificate with proof of identity).

The Jamaica Tourist Board desk here offers maps, brochures and friendly assistance. There's also an exchange booth directly through Immigration, but remember that US dollars are accepted everywhere, so you don't need to change money.

> **⊚ TIP**
>
> If the lines are moving, head on through Immigration and then come back to the tourist desk and/or currency exchange before you go downstairs to Customs.

The Customs process is generally speedy.

Take your stamped passport and immigration card downstairs to claim your luggage and proceed through Customs. You'll need to show your stamped Immigration card and declare any goods.

Once you're done with the formalities, you'll enter the bustling terminal's transportation area. If a driver is meeting you, he will probably be directly outside the doors with a sign. If your transportation has been arranged by one of the resorts, you'll find desks here. Red-capped porters offer their services for US50 cents per bag.

Red Stripe beer vendors are located just outside the door if you're ready to get into the Jamaican spirit.

Getting Around

Car & Jeep Rentals

Rental cars are pricey, and are available from most major rental companies. Renters must be at least 25 years old and possess a valid driver's license. A security deposit will need to be posted with either a credit card or cash. Service stations are open daily but accept only cash. The speed limit is 30 mph in town and 50 mph on the highways. Insurance costs $12 per day ($15 for jeeps) and is well worth the investment.

Montego Bay

MONTEGO BAY CAR RENTAL AGENCIES	
Budget	☎ 876-952-3838 (airport) ☎ 876-953-9765 (Ironshore)
Caribbean Car Rentals	☎ 876-952-0664 (19 Gloucester Ave.)
Central Rent-A-Car	☎ 876-952-3347 (25 Gloucester Ave.)
Discount Rent-A-Car	☎ 876-952-1943 (airport)
Island Car Rentals	☎ 876-952-5771 (airport) ☎ 876-953-9694 (Ironshore)
Thrifty Car Rental	☎ 876-952-5825 (28 Queen Dr. near airport)

Driving Times Within Jamaica

Kingston to Mandeville..... 1½ to 2 hrs
Montego Bay to Negril .... 1½ hrs
Montego Bay to Ocho Rios .. under 2 hrs
Ocho Rios to Port Antonio. under 2½ hrs
Ocho Rios to Kingston .... under 1½ hrs
Port Antonio to Kingston .. under 2 hrs

Driving Tips

In true British tradition, traffic keeps to the left side of the road. This can be confusing on your first day behind the wheel, so start off a little slower than usual. Most cars are right-hand drive, which will mean some adjustments for US drivers. (On our first excursion driving on the left side of the road we turned on the windshield wipers every time we tried to give a turn signal!)

Look RIGHT before crossing the street!

Taxis

Taxis are the most popular method of transportation for travelers, and can be summoned at any hotel, the airports, and most shopping areas.

◎ TIP

Not all of Jamaica's cabs are metered so agree on a price before entering the taxi.

If you need to call for a taxi, contact the official carrier: Jamaica Union of Travelers Association or **JUTA**, ☎ 876-952-0813 in Montego Bay.

Taxi rates vary, and you are charged by car, not by passenger. In general, fares are steep. We recently took a taxi from Wyndham Rose Hall to the Rose Hall Great House, a distance of just over a mile. The driver waited for us during our 45-minute tour. The taxi's price for the entire outing was US$16.

Many taxi drivers offer their services as island guides. If you accept a driver's offer for this service, be sure to agree on a price before the vehicle is put into gear. Expect to pay about US$50 and up for the services of a driver for a partial day.

Montego Bay

⊚ TIP

Look for red PPV license plates; these indicate legitimate taxis. Avoid those that do not have PPV plates – they are not legitimate cabs.

Bus Service

Bus travel is popular among Jamaicans. The vehicles (often minibuses) can be crowded and slow, and are generally not air-conditioned. Buses will stop anywhere along the route to pick up passengers. To catch one, stand by the side of the road with your arm outstretched; pat down with your hand when you see an oncoming bus.

Bus fare is cheap, (about US$1 for 30-40 miles).

Island Tours

 You'll find numerous tour companies, most operating through resort tour desks. Tour lengths vary from half-day to full day, although some multi-day tours are available.

Tour Companies

BLUE MOUNTAIN BICYCLE TOURS LTD.
Main Street, Ocho Rios
☎ 876-974-7075 or 974-7492, fax 876-974-0635

These downhill tours have been featured in many magazines and include brunch, lunch, refreshments and all bike equipment. The tours cover 18 miles (all downhill) through the Blue Mountains and the tropical rain forest.

CARIBIC
☎ 876-953-2600 or 979-9387, fax 876-979-3421
www.caribiconline.com

Is it legal for Americans to visit Cuba? No. Are these tours popular with Americans? Yes.

Cabric runs tours from Montego Bay to Cuba. Excursions include a flight from Montego Bay to Havana on Friday or Saturday; weekend packages are available to Havana or Varadero.

CS TOURS
66 Claude Clarke Ave.
☎876-953-2083

This company offers island sightseeing tours.

SAFARI TOURS
Mammee Bay
☎ 876-972-2639 or 876-919-7900
E-mail: Safari@toj.com
www.jamaica-irie.com/safari

Safari has several unique options. The all-day *Jeep Safari through Jamaica*, conducted on Monday and Wednesday, takes a look at island history, from Christopher Columbus to Bob Marley. The *Jeep Safari through the Blue Mountains*, on Thursday and Friday, travels high into the national park and includes a tour of Sangster's factory and a visit to the Bob Marley Museum in Kingston. The *Taste of Jamaica Tour*, held Monday through Saturday, is a half-day visit to Prospect Plantation, including horseback riding, a visit to Green Grotto Caves and a climb up Dunn's River Falls. The *Dunn's River Falls Bicycle Tour* (Mondays only) takes you on a downhill bike ride to Dunn's River Falls. Other excursions include horseback riding and river tubing (Monday through Saturday). One trip tackles river tubing in the morning and shopping in the afternoon.

SUNHOLIDAY
Holiday Village, Rose Hall
☎ 876-953-2837

This company offers sightseeing tours across Jamaica. You can sign up for one-day or multi-day tours.

Orientation

The town of Montego Bay lies on Jamaica's north coast, circling a semi-circular bay called, you guessed it, **Montego Bay**. It's likely that you'll enter the city at one of two places: the Sangster International Airport, located north of the city, or the cruise ship terminal, south of the city.

(Montego Bay)

Let's start with the **cruise terminal**, which lies on a peninsula named Freeport. The terminal itself offers a beautiful view of the city and its surrounding hills, and it's just a short drive north on Howard Cooke Boulevard into town, a route that takes you past some of the city's more industrial areas until you reach the **Crafts Market**, one of several. This is the downtown area. From the market, head east a few blocks to reach **A1**.

◎ TIP

Coming from the south, A1 is called Barnett Street, but as it reaches downtown it changes to St. James Street. Further north, as it crosses Sam Sharpe Square, it becomes Fort Street.

Continue north on this main thoroughfare and you'll soon reach the roundabout, a traffic circle. Here the road divides into Gloucester Avenue, left to the sea, and Queens Drive, right into the hills. **Queens Drive** is a beautiful route that offers great views; **Gloucester** is home to some of the city's top restaurants and bars, especially along a stretch fondly known as the **Hip Strip**.

Gloucester Avenue finally makes its way into an intersection with Sunset Boulevard, which then meets up with Queen's Drive at another roundabout at the entrance to Sangster International Airport. From here, Queen's Drive continues north as A1 (but just call it the main road and everyone will know what you're talking about) and on to the main resort area.

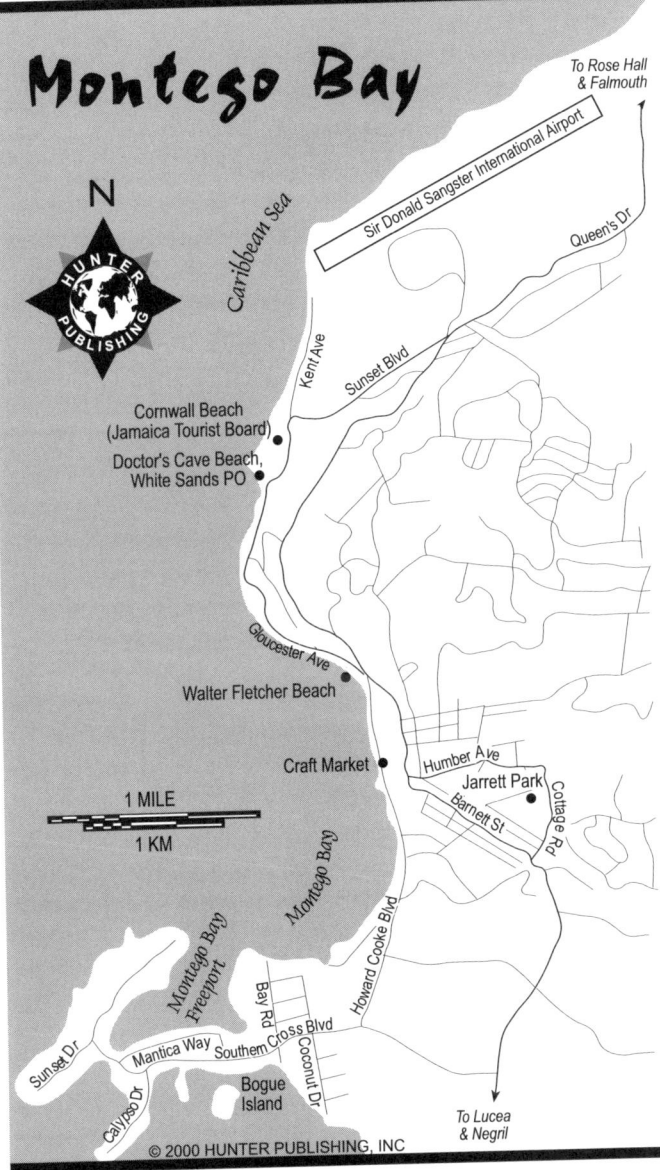

 # Best Places to Stay

Money Matters

 Room prices vary greatly with type of accommodation, location and time of year. High season (mid-December through mid-April) brings prices about 40% higher than in summer months.

Accommodations Price Scale

Prices are given in US dollars.

Deluxe. . . . . $300+
Expensive . . . . $200-$300
Moderate . . . . $100-$200
Inexpensive. . . . . Under $100

We've identified the all-inclusive properties in our listings.

Keep in mind as you compare prices that some resorts are all-inclusive (including all meals, drinks, tips, transfers and most activities in the price), while others are room only.

Resorts

COYABA BEACH RESORT AND CLUB
North Coast Highway at Mahoe Bay
☎ 876-953-9150, fax 876-953-2244
Reservations: ☎ 800-237-3237
www.elegantresorts.com
Expensive to Deluxe (All-inclusive optional)

This $10 million resort has the feel of an intimate inn, but it offers the amenities of a larger resort. Located on a shady stretch of beach, Coyaba is a good option if you're seeking the niceties and luxuries of an exclusive retreat. The hotel offers all-inclusive deals or EP only. The property features a plantation-style great house, which houses the main restaurant. Amenities include a freshwater pool, hot tub, massage, tennis, watersports and recreation room.

Coyaba is a small yet elegant property.

Guest rooms are light and airy, decorated in an elegant tropical style with mahogany furniture. You'll be greeted by a basket of banana bread, a sweet introduction to this special property. Amenities here include tennis, a dive shop, windsurfing, and a playground.

HALF MOON GOLF, TENNIS AND BEACH CLUB

North Coast Highway, 7 miles east of
Montego Bay
☎ 876-953-2211, fax 876-953-2731
Reservations: ☎ 800-237-3237
Deluxe

Half Moon is considered one of Jamaica's most elegant resorts, the place to be pampered. The resort offers a variety of room configurations, everything from large guest rooms and junior suites to villas that look like something right out of Beverly Hills, complete with sweeping staircases, maids and butlers. The black and white decor, like everything in the resort, is ultra chic.

The resort is a favorite with well-to-do Japanese vacationers, who feel right at home in rooms that

Montego Bay

offer Japanese-language periodicals and Japanese television channels in the rooms.

Ask for a golf cart for your stay at Half Moon if your room is a long way from the public areas.

Half Moon sprawls out across the island's north coast and you'll never feel crowded. Along with 13 tennis courts, 39 swimming pools, croquet, horseback riding, bikes, squash, numerous restaurants, a dive shop, kids' program, ultra-pricey shopping center, and even a hospital, you'll find a quiet nature reserve. The resort also now offers the David Leadbetter Golf Plan, with daily instruction from a David Leadbetter-certified instructor.

HOLIDAY INN SUNSPREE RESORT
North Coast Highway, 6 miles
east of Montego Bay
☎ 876-953-2485, fax 876-953-2840
Reservations: ☎ 800-HOLIDAY
Expensive to Deluxe (All-inclusive)

An excellent shopping area sits just across the street from the Holiday Inn.

Couples and families make up much of the clientele at this popular resort which has undergone many changes in the last several years. A $13 million facelift in 1995 transformed it into an all-inclusive property. The 523 guest rooms have all received an overhaul. Guests choose from watersports, tennis, volleyball, nearby golf, kids' programs, and more to fill their days here.

ROUND HILL HOTEL AND VILLAS
North Coast Highway, 8 miles
west of Montego Bay
☎ 876-956-7050, fax 876-956-7505
Reservations: ☎ 800-237-3237
www.roundhilljamaica.com
Deluxe

A favorite of the rich and famous set, Round Hill offers suites, traditional hotel rooms and 27 villas. Expensive and lavish, the villas include maid service (cook service is available as well), and many have a private pool.

Round Hill has a helipad for those arriving in style.

The resort includes numerous amenities, from tennis courts to a dive shop to windsurfing.

> ★ **DID YOU KNOW?**
>
> Round Hill was the location of many scenes in *How Stella Got Her Groove Back*.

Montego Bay

SANDALS MONTEGO BAY
Kent Avenue, near the airport
☎ 876-952-5510, fax 876-952-0816
Reservations: ☎ 800-726-3257
www.sandals.com
Deluxe (All-inclusive)

This popular couples-only resort does a huge amount of repeat business and is a great choice for those who want to be close to the airport, and you don't get much closer than this. Even though the planes buzz overhead, the property is very popular.

The staff at Sandals have made a game of the constant plane noises, encouraging couples to kiss each time a plane flies by.

Like other Sandals, guests at Sandals Montego Bay enjoy a "Stay at One, Dine at Six" policy. Guests can select from any of the 23 eating establishments in the Sandals chain. A desk at Sandals Montego Bay handles reservations at the other sister resorts; free shuttles are available to other Sandals located in Montego Bay.

Amenities here include five restaurants, numerous pools, tennis, racquetball, a dive shop, windsurfing and more. The resort's Sunshine Tennis program includes two hours of complimentary instruction per week with the visiting professional.

SANDALS ROYAL JAMAICAN
North Coast Highway
☎ 876-953-2231, fax 876-953-2788
Reservations: ☎ 800-726-3257
www.sandals.com
Expensive (All-inclusive)

What's the difference between Sandals Royal Jamaican and Sandals Montego Bay? Quite a bit. While Sandals Montego Bay boasts more of a party atmosphere, Sandals Royal Jamaican takes the more elegant, laid-back approach. In general, this property is much quieter than its cousin. We recently stayed in an elegant oceanfront deluxe room with a mahogany four-poster bed and two-level floor plan and thoroughly enjoyed it. On another visit, we came for dinner at Sandals' private island restaurant, known for its Indonesian fare and unbeatable night view of the city. It was a great dining experience.

Sandals Royal Jamaican is our favorite Sandals property on the island.

Amenities at the resort include four restaurants, numerous pools, tennis, a dive shop, windsurfing, concierge service and more.

SANDALS INN
Gloucester Avenue, in town
☎ 876-952-4140, fax 876-952-6913
Reservations: ☎ 800-726-3257
www.sandals.com
Expensive (All-inclusive)

Sandals Inn is the answer to the budget-conscious traveler who wants to enjoy a Sandals property. This small hotel isn't the sprawling beachfront resort usually associated with the Sandals chain, but it does have many of the same amenities. An all-inclusive package here takes care of transfers, activities, drinks and dining. Guests can also partake in the Sandals "Stay at One, Dine at Six" policy (with free transportation to the Mo Bay resorts). There's also a free shuttle that runs throughout the day to take you and yours (remember, this is a couples-only resort) from the inn to the larger Sandals Montego Bay or Sandals Royal Jamaican to enjoy beach fun. On-property facilities include tennis, pool and concierge service.

SUNSET BEACH RESORT AND SPA
Montego Freeport
☎ 876-979-8800, fax 876-953-6744
Expensive (All-inclusive)

This new 420-room resort is located on the Freeport peninsula. The property is divided into two sections: the 120-room, low-rise Beach Inn and the 300-room, 11-story Sunrise and Sunset Towers. The resort has an impressive list of facilities: three private beaches, three swimming pools, snorkeling, Sunfish, sailing, kayaking, windsurfing, paddle boats, Hobie Cats, jogging trails, beach volleyball, a fitness center and a supervised kids' program. Guests can use all of these without additional charge.

One of the sandy stretches at the Sunset Beach Inn is clothing-optional.

For late night fun, there's a disco as well as an electronic game casino. All meals are part of the package and guests have their choice of four restaurants, including Asian and Italian specialty restaurants. Six bars are located throughout the property. There's also a spa, although treatments are not part of the all-inclusive program.

TRYALL GOLF, TENNIS AND BEACH CLUB
North Coast Highway, 15 miles
west of Montego Bay
☎ 876-956-5660, fax 876-956-5658
Reservations: ☎ 800-238-5290
www.tryall-club.com
Deluxe

Tryall is home to one of the Caribbean's top golf courses.

If you're a golfer, you're probably already familiar with Tryall, a celebrity resort that has hosted many tournament games. This posh getaway includes everything you need to hole up and never leave if you so choose: a golf course, private villas with their own pools, tennis courts, dive shops, a driving range, you name it. You'll never feel crowded at this 2,200-acre property.

WYNDHAM ROSE HALL
North Coast Highway, east of Montego Bay
☎ 876-953-2650, fax 876-953-2617
Reservations: ☎ 800-996-3426
www.wyndham.com
Expensive (All-inclusive optional)

Don't miss the rum punches at Wyndham; they're some of the best on the island.

You can enjoy Wyndham Rose Hall on either a room-only basis or as an all-inclusive property. This sprawling resort is just a short drive from the airport, a real boon to those on a short vacation or traveling with restless kids. And, once you arrive, there's no need to worry about those kids remaining restless for long – Wyndham Rose Hall is home to a massive waterpark, a recent addition to the property. This 110,000-square-foot, $7 million water complex is called Sugar Mill Falls and comes complete with lagoons and a towering water slide. Guests can enjoy lazy river rafting among waterfalls scattered throughout the park.

This resort is presently undergoing a major upgrade, equipping its guest rooms with new furniture, carpeting, 27-inch TVs, movie channels, and more. The golf course is located directly across the street and soon golfers will be able to also use the nearby White Witch golf course, presently under construction by the Ritz-Carlton.

Wyndham Rose Hall is a great choice for golfers and families!

Montego Bay

Hotels

COMFORT INN AND
SUITES MONTEGO BAY
Rose Hall
☎ 876-953-3250, fax 876-953-3062
Reservations: ☎ 800-228-5150
www.choicecaribbean.com
Moderate (All-inclusive optional)

This 150-room hotel is the former SeaCastles and is a part of the Choice Hotels International group. It's situated on a small private beach.

The recently renovated property includes one- and two-bedroom units as well as studios. The all-inclusive package features three buffet meals daily, supervised kids' activities, non-motorized watersports, gratuities and taxes, house brand liquors and soft drinks, tennis, and daily entertainment. Every Friday the hotel offers a Jamaican night with local food and music.

The beach at the Comfort Inn is quite a walk from the rooms.

A shopping shuttle takes Comfort Inn guests to the craft village in Montego Bay.

RICHMOND HILL INN
Union Street
☎ 876-952-3859, fax 876-925-6106
Reservations: ☎ 800-423-4095
Moderate

A trip to Richmond Hill Inn is like visiting your grandmother's house: you're a little afraid that you're going to knock something over; you really wish it weren't so fussy, but you love the way you get treated. The rooms here have seen fresher days, but still the view is special: straight out at Montego Bay and the sea from high atop the hill.

★ DID YOU KNOW?

Richmond Hill has a long history, dating back to the 1790s, when it was the property of the Dewars of Scotch whisky fame.

Small Hotels

LETHE ESTATE
20 minutes west of Montego Bay
on the North Coast Highway
☎ 876-956-4920, fax 876-956-4927
Expensive

This quiet getaway isn't really in Mo Bay, but is a beautiful drive from the city. This property is for those who really want to get away from it all and immerse themselves in the flora and fauna of Jamaica. Away from the beach, this small property is tucked on the banks of the river near the village of Lethe, west of Montego Bay.

"It is not for everyone. It is not for the first-time traveler unless they are looking to hibernate," says co-owner Doreen Tulloch. "I'm there for guests, but not in the way. I don't want to take your money as an all-inclusive because I want you to go out and see Jamaica. I'm not hiding Jamaica. I'm looking for the traveler who really wants to know Jamaica."

The Lethe Estate is situated in a beautiful, unspoiled setting.

Guests don't need to worry about leaving amenities, however, because the inn includes a gourmet restaurant, pool, tennis and plush rooms. A top daytime activity here is floating on a bamboo raft down the river under a canopy of forest. Guests enjoy a free shuttle to the beach and to shopping areas daily.

Montego Bay

VERNEY'S TROPICAL RESORT
Leader Avenue, in town
☎ 876-952-2875 or 876-952-8628, fax 876-979-2944
Inexpensive

This 27-room inn is an excellent place to find true Jamaican hospitality. Rooms are nothing fancy, but owners Kathleen and Earnest Sterling are on property like round-the-clock concierges. Need a babysitter? Kathleen will find you one. Want to know where to shop for spices? Just ask. You'll feel like part of the family. "We really believe in personal service because once you are away from home it is good to know someone cares," says Kathleen. The hotel's Kit Kat restaurant is a favorite recommendation with hotels in Montego Bay whenever they're asked for real Jamaican cooking.

Verney's offers a nice, local atmosphere.

Best Places to Eat

After a day of watersports or beach fun, many travelers look to the island's fine dining as the evening's entertainment.

In the restaurant department, Mo Bay has definitely got something for everyone, whether your tastes run toward fresh island seafood or cuisines from around the world. Some of the island's restaurants have received many accolades over the last few years and gained quite a following among the many returning guests who frequent the island; others are new on the scene. Some are especially suited for couples looking for a special night out; others welcome families with dishes that please even the pickiest eater in the group.

Money Matters

Visa, Mastercard, Amex, Diners Club and Access are commonly accepted; Discover is accepted at some establishments.

◎ TIP

Most restaurants add a 15% gratuity to the bill, so make sure you don't inadvertently tip twice.

Expect to pay about US$35-55 per person for a three-course meal with wine in one of the island's finest restaurants. Travelers should expect to spend about US$6-10 for a casual lunch or dinner. Fast food lunches or snacks can be obtained for about US$3-7 per person.

All-Inclusive Dining

If you see a restaurant designated as "all-inclusive" in the price listing, this is a restaurant located on an all-inclusive resort. Guests at the resort can dine there as part of their package. But what if you're not staying there?

Have no fear. We've included the local telephone number of the resort so just give them a call and ask about purchasing a day pass. Most Jamaican all-inclusives sell both day and evening passes which allow non-guests to come on-property and enjoy the amenities. Everyone comes out a winner. You get to try a new restaurant and the resort tempts you to book your next vacation with them.

Montego Bay

For dining, we've set up a price scale based on a three-course dinner including appetizer or soup, an entrée, dessert and coffee. Cocktails and wine are extra.

Dining Price Scale

Prices are per person in US dollars.

Expensive. . . . . $40+ per person
Moderate . . . . $25-$40
Inexpensive. . . . . Under $25

Fine Dining

AMBROSIA

Wyndham Rose Hall
☎ 876-953-2605
Expensive

Ambrosia specialties are lobster Provençale and lamb kebabs.

Located at the golf club across the street from Wyndham Rose Hall, this elegant eatery features Mediterranean cuisine served in a beautiful garden setting. Set off with tiny white lights, the dining area is a good spot for a romantic dinner out. Closed Wednesdays.

BALI HAI

Sandals Royal Jamaican
North Coast Highway
☎ 876-953-2231
All-inclusive

At night, Bali Hai offers one of the best views of Montego Bay's city lights.

We've dined several times at this restaurant located on a small island off the beach from Sandals Royal Jamaica. After a quick ride aboard the launch for one of the two nightly seatings, diners are treated to a fixed menu featuring spicy Indonesian cuisine.

Appetizer offerings include lumpia goreng, a spring roll stuffed with cabbage, bamboo shoots and shrimp, and soto ajam dawa, a Javanese-style chicken broth with chicken and spring onion. Multiple entrées are served on hot bricks and include tjap tjai (chicken with mixed vegetables), daging bali (spiced beef cooked in soya sauce), fkan kuning (trout fillet steamed in coconut milk), sambal goreng kentang (spicy potato sticks), babi ketjap (porkloin simmered in a ginger sauce) and tumis buncis (stringbean stewed in coconut milk). A dinner here is a memorable experience and one we'd highly recommend.

BELFIELD 1794
Barnett Estate
☎ 876-952-2382
Expensive

This elegant restaurant, located on the 3,000-acre Barnett Estate near Montego Bay on Granville Main Road, is operated by Elegant Resorts International. The open-air restaurant features a view of the city and a menu that combines a taste of Jamaica and the Caribbean.

After your meal, enjoy a leisurely stroll over to the great house. The restored historic house is open to visitors; guided tours are available before or after dinner.

Menu selections include spicy ackee tomato salsa on smoked marlin, plantation salad, jerk pork Belfield, steamed fish Port Royal, and sweet potato pudding.

CUCINA ROMANA
Sandals Montego Bay
Kent Avenue
☎ 876-952-5510
All-inclusive

This fine dining restaurant serves Italian cuisine in an Italian setting. Start with antipasti from the buffet, but save room for entrées such as pesce spada alla griglia (pan-grilled swordfish steak), pollo al rosmarino (chicken roasted in olive oil, onion, rosemary, potatoes and red wine), and ossobuco Milanese (veal shank served with saffron rice).

JULIA'S
Bogue Hill
☎ 876-952-1772
Expensive

Reservations are required & dressy clothing is recommended at Julia's.

One of Jamaica's most lauded eateries, Julia's is a favorite with the celebrity set. A taste of the offerings and it's easy to see why. Italian dishes fill the menu and often the owner comes out to sing.

LETHE ESTATE
20 minutes west of Montego Bay
on the North Coast Highway
☎ 876-956-4920
Expensive

Dress is casually elegant at Lethe Estate.

Gourmet dining on dishes that include many local ingredients. A relaxing meal here is the perfect end to a day at the Lethe Estate.

MARGUERITES
Gloucester Avenue
☎ 876-952-4777
Expensive

Reservations are suggested at Marguerites.

For all the casualness of its next door neighbor, Margueritaville, Marguerites offers something elegant and special. The two eateries may be yards apart, but in atmosphere they might as well be at opposite ends of the island. The specialty of the house at this seaside restaurant is the flambéed dishes, such as Tijuana shrimp flambéed in tequila and Grand Marnier.

NORMA'S AT THE WHARF HOUSE

Reading, west of Montego Bay

☎ 876-979-2745

Expensive

Norma's (like the Kingston restaurant of the same name) is known for its nouvelle Jamaica cuisine, all served up in an historic setting. The restaurant is the creation of Norma Shirley, one of Jamaica's most noted chefs.

Norma's has been featured in Bon Appetit and Food and Wine magazines.

THE OLEANDER ROOM

Sandals Montego Bay

Kent Avenue

☎ 876-952-5510

All-inclusive

This is the most elegant eatery at Sandals Montego Bay, a Georgian-style restaurant that serves Jamaican cuisine with a gourmet twist, all in a refined white-glove atmosphere. Seatings are 6 pm to 9 pm. Long pants and collared shirts are required; reservations are also necessary.

Menu selections at the Oleander Room include: red snapper escovitch, pork cutlet grilled with pimento seeds and Jamaican steamed fish.

THE PAVILLION

Sandals Royal Jamaican

North Coast Highway

☎ 876-953-2231

All-inclusive

We enjoyed an elegant, open-air dinner at this restaurant many years ago on one of our first trips to Jamaica. It still provides excellent dining experience for couples today. Long pants and collared

Montego Bay

shirts are required; reservations are also necessary.

Menu selections at the Pavillion include: Chef Wood's jerk chicken, poached filet of tilapia filled with callaloo, and roast porkloin escovitch.

ROUND HILL
West of Montego Bay on North Coast Highway
☎ 876-956-7050
Expensive

Round Hill is one of the island's dressiest restaurants.

Dining at Round Hill is an elegant experience in which you are served by candlelight under the stars. Dishes such as grilled mahi mahi with fennel and orange salad, duck and sausage cassoulet, or crab salad with fresh coconut are on offer. Fresh seafood is featured nightly. Saturday is the dressiest night at Round Hill; jacket and tie are required. Mondays are casual with a beach barbecue and bonfire. On Wednesdays, dinner is à la carte, while on Friday they feature a Jamaican menu followed by a Jamaican folkloric performance. After dinner on Saturday, Tuesday, and Thursday nights, guests enjoy dancing to Billy Cook's Jazz, the house band.

Informal Dining

KIT KAT RESTAURANT
Verney's Tropical Resort
Leader Avenue
☎ 876-952-2875
Inexpensive to Moderate

Kit Kat menu selections include: curried goat, breadfruit and jerk chicken.

This delightful restaurant offers visitors a real taste of Jamaican home cooking. It is located in the modest Verney's Tropical Resort, a small property with a hilltop view of the city. The open-air restaurant features genuine Jamaican dishes (with real amounts of Jamaican spice, not watered-down versions for tourist tastes).

MARGUERITAVILLE CARIBBEAN BAR AND GRILL
Gloucester Avenue
☎ 876-952-4777
Moderate

Margueritaville offers a fun, casual atmosphere.

You don't just visit Margueritaville for the food – a stop here is more for the party atmosphere. Casual dining is the order of the day: American favorites like burgers and pizza top the list.

But the food is just an excuse to come use the extensive facilities, which include a waterslide that plummets from the upstairs bar right into the sea and giant TV screens.

THE NATIVE
29 Gloucester Avenue
☎ 876-979-2769
Moderate

Tucked under a sprawling poinciana tree, this open-air eatery is a wonderful place to step away from the packaged fun of the resorts and watch Montego Bay life roll by.

Reservations are required for dinner at The Native.

We came to The Native for a lunch buffet, an impressive spread of salads, rice and peas, jerk chicken, snapper, and other island delights. Offered every Friday and Sunday, this noon buffet is popular with vacationers and locals alike. And if you can't make it for the buffet, order up the

Montego Bay

Boonoonoonos Platter for a sample of lots of local specialties.

THE PELICAN
Gloucester Avenue
☎ 876-952-3171
Moderate

This popular restaurant has attracted diners for over three decades and many local business people start their workday with a traditional Jamaican breakfast right here. Jamaican dishes appear on the lunch and dinner menu as well.

THE PORK PIT
27 Gloucester Avenue
☎ 876-952-1046
Inexpensive

The Pork Pit offers a real taste of Jamaica!

Jerk chicken, spare ribs, steam roast fish, sweet potatoes, roast yam, festival and cold coconut water star at this fast-food eatery that's a favorite with local diners. Located across from Walter Fletcher Beach. Order up a plate and then grab a place at one of the picnic tables on the open patio for a real Jamaican meal. Like the menu here, seating is simple and no frills. However, for real Jamaican jerk, this is the place to go in Montego Bay.

RICHMOND HILL INN
Union Street
☎ 876-952-3859
Moderate to Expensive

Wear something dressy for dinner at the Richmond Hill Inn.

The view from this restaurant alone makes the trip to Richmond Hill Inn worthwhile. The open-air restaurant serves up a variety of continental and Jamaican fare, all enjoyed with a beautiful view of the city lights and the bay.

THE ROYAL STOCKS
ENGLISH PUB AND STEAKHOUSE
Half Moon Village
☎ 876-953-9770
Moderate

Royal Stocks offers a fun pub atmosphere.

We recently enjoyed a lunch here while attending a Jamaican tourism convention held at the Half Moon Conference Centre, just steps away. Both indoor and outside seating are available in this traditional English pub that serves steaks, lobster and seafood as well as pub fare. The bar has a full selection of traditional ales. When you're ready for fun, there's a sports bar (with darts and skittles). Call for free transportation if you're not staying on property.

SAKURA JAPANESE RESTAURANT
Half Moon Village
North Coast Highway
☎ 876-953-9686
Expensive

The black and white decor of this restaurant, in keeping with that throughout Half Moon, hints at the elegance found inside. Proof of the many cuisines Jamaica offers, this restaurant features hibachi grill-top cooking right at your table. With his flying knives, the chef will prepare a meal of seafood, steak or chicken that's as good as the show itself. Reservations required.

The round-trip transportation from your local hotel to Sakura is provided free of charge.

Montego Bay

SEAGRAPE TERRACE
Half Moon Hotel, North Coast Highway
☎ 876-953-2211
Moderate to Expensive

This open-air eatery sits right on the beach and serves up Caribbean cuisine. Both buffet and à la carte service are available at lunch; dinner is à la carte only. In the evenings, the atmosphere is lively with dancing and floor shows. A Jamaican beach barbecue is offered on Monday and Friday nights and you can try local specialties then dance to the sounds of a steel pan band.

TAPAS
Corniche Road, behind the Coral Cliff Hotel
☎ 876-952-2988
Moderate to Expensive

We recommend you book a table ahead of time at Tapas.

The name here suggests the strong influence of Spanish cuisine found on the menu, which also features Caribbean dishes. Don't miss the tapas, especially the smoked duck and lamb with jerk sauce.

TOKYO JOE'S
Sandals Montego Bay
Kent Avenue
☎ 876-952-5510
All-inclusive

This dinner-only restaurant (which is closed on Fridays) serves Asian dishes. Start with miso soup or dim sum (select from beef satay, crispy wonton, pork dumplings or shrimp) or create a specialty salad at the salad bar. Entrées are cooked to order.

TOWN HOUSE
16 Church Street
☎ 876-952-2660
Moderate to Expensive

Built in 1765, this restaurant and tavern features brick walls decorated with local artwork. You can dine inside or on the verandah. Offerings run the gamut from red snapper papillot, spare ribs and stuffed lobster to shrimp, steaks, pastas and Jamaican dishes, including many curried entrées. Open from Monday through Saturday for lunch and daily for dinner, the restaurant offers free round-trip transportation from local hotels.

Reservations are required for dinner at the Town House.

Montego Bay

THE VINEYARD
Coyaba Beach Resort and Club
☎ 876-953-9150
Moderate to Expensive

This restaurant, decorated like a trellised garden, features Caribbean and continental dishes for breakfast and dinner.

Make advance reservations for dinner at The Vineyard.

Sunup to Sundown

Montego Bay can be as crazy or as lazy as you wish. Spend your day on the beach or jump up and head out in search of adventure – the choice is yours.

Beaches

Montego Bay is home to several beautiful beaches; any beachfront property will have a great slice of sand. Most vacationers use the beach at their property; if you visit the public beaches expect to see numerous vendors offering everything from hair braiding to jerk pork to "something special." Some of the most notable and best-known public beaches in the city are:

Cornwall Beach. A favorite with locals. There's plenty to do at this action-packed beach, including watersports.

Doctor's Cave Beach. This downtown beach is really the birthplace of Montego Bay's tourism. The waters in this cave were said to be curative and drew many travelers to bathe here. Today the beach has more of a spring break feel and is always busy.

Walter Fletcher Beach. Another downtown beach, Walter Fletcher is a favorite with local and vacationing families because of its calm waters.

Scuba Diving

Montego Bay is the home of the first marine park in Jamaica. The **Montego Bay Marine Park** (☎ 876-952-5619) was established to protect the natural resources of this underwater wonderland; a quick look at the area and it's easy to see the treasures that lie beneath the surface. You can explore the region aboard one of the semi-submersibles (see *Unique Tours*, below) or, if you're a certified diver, check it out with one of these operators:

DIVE OPERATORS	
Fun Divers, Wyndham Rose Hall	☎ 876-953-2650
Jamaqua Dive Centre	☎ 876-973-4845
Poseidon Divers, Reading Reef Club	☎ 876-952-3624
North Coast Marine Sports, Half Moon	☎ 876-953-2211
Sandals Inn	☎ 876-952-4140
Sandals Montego Bay	☎ 876-979-9130
Sandals Royal Jamaican	☎ 876-953-2231

Montego Bay

Snorkeling

Most resorts in Montego Bay offer snorkel excursions, opportunities to take a boat just offshore and enjoy a reef dive. Even first-time snorkelers can look at colorful corals, graceful fans and fish that include friendly sergeant majors, butterfly fish and shy damselfish. You don't have to be an expert to enjoy these excursions.

Sailing

Rhapsody
204 Chatwick Plaza, Queens Drive
☎ 876-979-0102

This sailing cruise can be booked through most hotel tour desks or you can call the

office directly. Cruises include day sails, snorkel cruises and sunset sails, as well as private charters.

Horseback Riding

Riding a horse through the surf is a favorite Mo Bay activity. There are also many beautiful trail rides.

☺ TIP

We suggest morning rides. By mid-day, temperatures away from the beach trade winds can get a little toasty.

ROCKY POINT STABLES
North Coast Highway, next to Half Moon
☎ 876-953-2286, fax 876-953-9489

This well-respected stable offers horseback rides and lessons as well as pony rides. Dressage and show jumping lessons are available, as are polo lessons (arena polo is played seasonally Tuesdays at 4:30 pm). Several organized rides are also offered. *The Jungle Jaunt* (45 minutes, scheduled for 9 am, 10 am and 3 pm) is for beginners, starting with a short lesson in the arena then a trek through the Half Moon Nature Reserve. *The Tryall Trail* (90 minutes, scheduled for 9 am, 10 am and 3 pm) travels along bridle paths to the village of Tryall, back through the Half Moon Golf Course. The *Trail and Treat* option (2½ hours,

English saddles are used at Rocky Point. Helmets are also supplied.

9 am only) combines a ride into the mountains to Tryall with a dip in the ocean.

Fishing

Try your luck reeling in a marlin, tuna, kingfish or bonito with a half- or full-day charter. Prices aren't cheap; expect to pay about $300 for a half-day cruise, although that includes just about everything your group will need for the excursion, including equipment.

FISHING OPERATORS	
No Problem	☎ 876-995-2912
North Coast Marine at Half Moon	☎ 876-953-9266
Rhapsody	☎ 876-979-0104
Seaworld	☎ 876-953-2188

Golf

Montego Bay is home to several of Jamaica's most noted golf courses. Rolling hills provide the perfect challenge and several of the courses offer beautiful sea views at some holes.

Expect to pay US$10-30 for a golf cart as well as US$5-15 for a mandatory caddy. Clubs rent for US$5-20.

Rates are lower during the summer.

HALF MOON GOLF CLUB
☎ 876-953-3105

The course at Half Moon was designed by Robert Trent Jones, Jr.

This 18-hole course is the home of the Red Stripe Pro Am and is considered one of the island's best. Rates run $95. Facilities include a clubhouse, restaurant, bar and pro shop. Par 72.

IRONSHORE
☎ 876-953-2800

Ironshore was designed by the Canadian Robert Motte.

Links-style golf is the attraction of this 18-hole course. Rates run $45; facilities include a clubhouse, restaurant, bar and pro shop. Par 72.

TRYALL
☎ 876-956-5681

The course at Tryall was designed by Ralph Plummer.

This 18-hole course is one of the best in the Caribbean (some even say the world). Built on a 19th-century sugar plantation, the course is an official PGA tour approved course and is the site of many tournaments. Facilities include a clubhouse, restaurant, bar and pro shop. Rates run $40-$60 for guests, $100-$125 for those not registered at Tryall. Par 70.

◎ TIP

Even if you're not a golfer, don't miss the course's water wheel next to the main road. It's a great photo spot.

WYNDHAM ROSE HALL
☎ 876-953-2650

This 18-hole course has hosted many invitational tournaments and is well known by golfers and non-golfers alike because of its location on the grounds of the historic Rose Hall great house. Rates run $50-$60. Facilities include a clubhouse, restaurant, bar and pro shop. Par 72.

White Witch Course Under Construction

At press time, construction was underway on the White Witch golf course, adjacent to the Wyndham Rose Hall course and the Rose Hall great house. Look for the course, part of the new Ritz Carlton, to draw a lot of attention.

Tennis

Most resorts offer several tennis courts, many lit for night play. Tennis is, of course, most popular during the morning hours before the heat drives all but the most dedicated players off the courts.

Unique Tours

ACCOMPONG MAROON TOUR
☎ 876-979-0308
Hours: 8 am - 6 pm daily
Admission

The Maroons were escaped slaves who headed for the hills in the 17th century and were never recaptured. Today the Maroons live as their own society, separate from Jamaican law, with their own elected officials and rules in a remote region of Jamaica known as Cockpit Country. We flew over this area one time in a small four-seater traveling from Kingston to Negril and were amazed at its size, devoid of roads and marked by only a few homes here and there. The area is extremely hilly and verdant, little changed from the days when the original Maroons made their homes here.

The "capital" of the region is the community of **Accompong**. The tour makes a visit in this unique town for a look at its historic buildings and residents, who are considered the greatest herbalists in Jamaica.

APPLETON EXPRESS
Book with your hotel tour desk
Hours: 8:30 am - 4 pm Tuesday through Thursday
Admission

The Appleton Express is an air-conditioned bus that travels from Mo Bay to the **Appleton Rum Distillery** on the south side of the island. (If you traveled to Jamaica a decade ago, you may remember that the Appleton Express was formerly a train that took day trippers across the island. Sadly, the train no longer runs. Ahh... the good old days.)

Today's tour includes a stop at the Appleton Rum Distillery for a tour and a tasting (every visitor gets a complimentary bottle; children get soft drinks). The tour also makes a stop at **Ipswich Caves**.

LETHE PLANTATION JITNEY TOUR
20 minutes west of Montego Bay
on the North Coast Highway
☎ 876-952-0527
Hours: 9 am - 4 pm daily
Admission

Located 20 minutes from Mo Bay, the Lethe Plantation runs a popular tour that looks at the Great River valley. Owned by Francis and Doreen Tulloch of Lethe Estate (see *Intimate Inns*, above) and Lethe Mountain Rafting, this attraction includes a reconstructed tropical village with freshwater fish ponds, a tropical garden, and a look at a banana plantation from an open-air jitney.

LETHE MOUNTAIN VALLEY RAFTING
20 minutes west of Montego Bay,
North Coast Highway
☎ 876-956-4920-6
Hours: 9 am - 5 pm daily
Admission

This is the epitome of relaxation. Climb aboard a bamboo raft and take a one-hour float down the tranquil Great River. The ride is quiet and hassle-free (no vendors here, in contrast to the Rio Grande rafting excursion) and you're welcome to take a dip in the river if you like. The ride isn't cheap (about $36 per raft) but very relaxing.

Be sure to bring cash to tip your raftsman.

MARTHA BRAE RIVER RAFTING
☎ 876-954-5168 or book through
your hotel tour desk
Hours: Opens daily at 9 am; closes at sunset
Admission

Like the mountain rafting at Lethe and the Rio Grande, this attraction features rafting down a

Montego Bay

tranquil river (the Martha Brae). The ride lasts about 1½ hours.

Nature Tours

MOBAY UNDERSEA TOURS
Gloucester Avenue, downtown Montego Bay
☎ 876-979-2281
Open daily
Admission

An underwater tour is a good rainy day activity.

This is not a true submarine but actually sort of a deep glass-bottom boat with portholes. The tours depart from Margueritaville and you are shuttled out to the vessel. A short walk down the stairs and you'll be in the glass hull surrounded by viewing windows that look onto Montego Bay's Marine Park. Sponges, corals and numerous fish, (even a few turtles during our visit!) make the ride spectacular. The ride isn't inexpensive (US$30), but worth the cost for non-divers.

This is a fun and educational attraction that's a must, especially if you're not a scuba diver or snorkeler.

SHARKEY'S TOURS
Pier One
Tours at 11, 1:30 and 4
☎ 876-971-1049
Admission

This semi-sub offers views of marine life for up to 48 passengers. Tours include a sunset cruise as well as tours of the marine sanctuary.

Sights & Attractions

BARNETT ESTATE
Granville Main Road
☎ 876-952-2382, fax 876-952-6342
Open daily
Admission

This plantation tour is one of the island's best. The Barnett Estate, a longtime farm, has grown everything from sugar cane to coconuts and you can sample its offerings during a one-hour horseback tour.

BELVEDERE ESTATE
Chester Castle
☎ 876-956-7310
Admission

Take a peek back at the plantation days with this heritage tour.

BOB MARLEY EXPERIENCE
Half Moon Shopping Village
North Coast Highway
Hours: 10 am - 6 pm daily
Free

This new attraction features a 68-seat theater where you can watch a documentary on the life and works of reggae great Bob Marley. The film runs several times daily. The largest part of the attraction is a huge shop filled with Marley memorabilia – CDs, books, t-shirts. The shop claims to have the largest collection of Marley gifts in the Caribbean.

The Bob Marley Experience is a great free attraction and a good rainy day activity.

Montego Bay

CROYDON IN THE MOUNTAINS
Located 20 miles into the interior near the town of
Catadupa in St. James (take B6 out of town)
Hours: 8:30 am - 5:30 pm daily;
tours from 10:30 am - 3:30 pm
☎ 876-979-8267
Admission

Croydon tours include a Jamaican lunch served with Blue Mountain coffee.

This 132-acre working pineapple and coffee plantation offers half-day estate tours. The property was the birthplace of Samuel Sharpe, a national hero on this island. Sharpe lead a slave rebellion in 1831 that helped bring about the abolition of slavery. You can learn about the preparation of coffee, honey, pineapples and more.

DOCTOR'S CAVE BEACH
☎ 876-952-2566
Open daily
Admission

In 1906 Dr. Alexander James McCatty stated that the waters off this beach had all kinds of health benefits (there are minerals in the water). The doctor donated his property to start a bathing club; access was through a cave that was later destroyed by a hurricane in 1932. Today, this spot is still called Doctor's Cave Beach and is a favorite with locals as well as with travelers staying in the downtown hotels.

GREENWOOD GREAT HOUSE
North Coast Hwy, 15 miles east of Montego Bay
☎ 876-953-1077
Hours: 9 am - 6 pm daily
Admission

After your tour of Greenwood, take a break at the pub here.

This was once the home of the Barrett family (as in Elizabeth Barrett Browning). Tours here include a look at the finery enjoyed by the plantation families.

ROCKLANDS FEEDING STATION
Anchovy
☎ 876-952-2009
Feeding times: 3:30 and 5 pm daily
Admission

This is the home of Lisa Salmon, 93, Jamaica's best-known ornithologist. Her home/bird sanctuary is surrounded by clouds of grassquits, saffron finches, and, most especially, hummingbirds.

Salmon moved to the verdant hillside in April 1952 and found this site, a short drive from the beaches of Montego Bay, filled with feathered friends. Through the years, Salmon worked as a bird advocate, achieving a limit on Jamaica's bird hunting season. In 1959 she opened the bird sanctuary and since that time travelers from around the world have hand-fed the regular guests of this bird diner. Tiny finches flutter around outstretched palms filled with birdseed, while fast-as-lightning hummingbirds drink from a hand-held bottle of sugar water.

Rocklands is one of the island's best eco-tourism attractions!

ROSE HALL
North Coast Highway
☎ 876-953-2323
Hours: 9 am - 6 pm daily
Admission

Rose Hall is the best-known great house in Jamaica and is an easy afternoon visit for Montego Bay guests. This was once the home of the notorious Annie Palmer, better known as the White Witch.

Montego Bay

The White Witch

As the story goes, Annie was born in 1802 in England to an English mother and Irish father. At the age of 10, her family moved to Haiti, and soon her parents died of yellow fever. Annie was adopted by a Haitian voodoo priestess and soon became skilled in the practice of voodoo. Annie moved to Jamaica, married, and built Rose Hall, an enormous plantation spanning 6,600 acres with over 2,000 slaves. According to legend, Annie murdered several of her husbands and her slave lovers. To know more about the tales of Rose Hall, read the novel *The White Witch of Rose Hall*.

After the Rose Hall tour, stop by the pub for a taste of rum or a local beer.

Guided tours take you to the ballroom, dining room, Annie's bedroom and grave. The gift shop displays photographs of what many believe are ghostly apparitions, shots taken in the bedrooms.

★ NOTE

Near Rose Hall, an exclusive resort is being built: the $113 million Ritz Carlton Rose Hall. The 430-room property is due to open in early 2000.

Shop Till You Drop

Shopping Centers

SANGSTER INTERNATIONAL AIRPORT

Unlike many Caribbean airports, you'll find a good selection of shops at Sangster. Beyond the security checkpoint you can shop for duty-free goods, coffees and more at shops, including the following.

- ◎ **Bijoux Jewellers** for duty-free jewelry (two shops).

- ◎ **Celebrate Jamaica** sells sweets (don't miss the Tia Maria-filled chocolates!).

- ◎ **Coffee and Spice** offers a final taste of Jamaica to take home.

- ◎ **Sunshine Liquors**.

- ◎ **The Perfume Shop**.

- ◎ **Jamaica Farewell** sells duty-free liquor and tobacco products.

- ◎ **Charlene's Books and Sundries** has a good selection of local books, including some cookbooks.

- ◎ **Things Jamaican** sells weavings, ceramics, leather goods, bamboo souvenirs and other local crafts.

Montego Bay

- The **Gallery of Caribbean Art** offers paintings and carvings.
- **Island Creations Craft and Linen Store**
- **Maid in Jamaica** has more locally produced crafts.
- **Flowers and Fruits** features a good selection of jams, jellies and juices made from tropical fruits.

HALF MOON SHOPPING VILLAGE

In the Half Moon Resort, this shopping area is one of the island's best, both for its high-end goods such as designer watches and fine jewelry, as well as for its clothing. The open-air village sits adjacent to the resort's conference center and is also home to several restaurants and the Bob Marley Experience (see above).

HOLIDAY VILLAGE SHOPPING CENTRE

This collection of inexpensive shops sells everything from Bob Marley t-shirts to rasta tams, wood carvings to straw baskets. Liquor stores offer local rums, liqueurs and coffees. Across from Holiday Inn SunSpree.

Money Matters

The rate of exchange changes daily but at press time these were the conversion rates.

CURRENCY CONVERSION CHART	
US$ is equal to J$	*J$ is equal to US$*
1 ~ ~ ~ ~ ~ ~ ~ ~ ~ 37.50	10 ~ ~ ~ ~ ~ ~ ~ ~ ~ ~ .27
2 ~ ~ ~ ~ ~ ~ ~ ~ ~ 75.00	20 ~ ~ ~ ~ ~ ~ ~ ~ ~ ~ .53
3 ~ ~ ~ ~ ~ ~ ~ ~ 112.50	30 ~ ~ ~ ~ ~ ~ ~ ~ ~ ~ .80
4 ~ ~ ~ ~ ~ ~ ~ ~ 150.00	40~ ~ ~ ~ ~ ~ ~ ~ ~ ~ 1.07
5 ~ ~ ~ ~ ~ ~ ~ ~ 187.50	50~ ~ ~ ~ ~ ~ ~ ~ ~ ~ 1.33
6 ~ ~ ~ ~ ~ ~ ~ ~ 225.00	60~ ~ ~ ~ ~ ~ ~ ~ ~ ~ 1.60
7 ~ ~ ~ ~ ~ ~ ~ ~ 262.50	70~ ~ ~ ~ ~ ~ ~ ~ ~ ~ 1.87
8 ~ ~ ~ ~ ~ ~ ~ ~ 300.00	80~ ~ ~ ~ ~ ~ ~ ~ ~ ~ 2.13
9 ~ ~ ~ ~ ~ ~ ~ ~ 337.50	90~ ~ ~ ~ ~ ~ ~ ~ ~ ~ 2.40
10 ~ ~ ~ ~ ~ ~ ~ ~ 375.00	100~ ~ ~ ~ ~ ~ ~ ~ ~ ~ 2.67
15 ~ ~ ~ ~ ~ ~ ~ ~ 562.50	150~ ~ ~ ~ ~ ~ ~ ~ ~ ~ 4.00
20 ~ ~ ~ ~ ~ ~ ~ ~ 750.00	200~ ~ ~ ~ ~ ~ ~ ~ ~ ~ 5.33
30 ~ ~ ~ ~ ~ ~ ~ ~ 1125.00	300~ ~ ~ ~ ~ ~ ~ ~ ~ ~ 8.00
40~ ~ ~ ~ ~ ~ ~ ~ 1500.00	400 ~ ~ ~ ~ ~ ~ ~ ~ ~ 10.67
50 ~ ~ ~ ~ ~ ~ ~ ~ 1875.00	500 ~ ~ ~ ~ ~ ~ ~ ~ ~ 13.33
60~ ~ ~ ~ ~ ~ ~ ~ 2250.00	600 ~ ~ ~ ~ ~ ~ ~ ~ ~ 16.00
70~ ~ ~ ~ ~ ~ ~ ~ 2625.00	700 ~ ~ ~ ~ ~ ~ ~ ~ ~ 18.67
80~ ~ ~ ~ ~ ~ ~ ~ 3000.00	800 ~ ~ ~ ~ ~ ~ ~ ~ ~ 21.33
90~ ~ ~ ~ ~ ~ ~ ~ 3375.00	900 ~ ~ ~ ~ ~ ~ ~ ~ ~ 24.00
100~ ~ ~ ~ ~ ~ ~ ~ 3750.00	1,000 ~ ~ ~ ~ ~ ~ ~ ~ ~ 27.00
200~ ~ ~ ~ ~ ~ ~ ~ 7500.00	2,000 ~ ~ ~ ~ ~ ~ ~ ~ ~ 53.00
300~ ~ ~ ~ ~ ~ ~ ~ 11,250.00	4,000 ~ ~ ~ ~ ~ ~ ~ 107.00
400~ ~ ~ ~ ~ ~ ~ 15,000.00	6,000 ~ ~ ~ ~ ~ ~ ~ 160.00
500~ ~ ~ ~ ~ ~ ~ 18,750.00	8,000 ~ ~ ~ ~ ~ ~ ~ 213.00

Montego Bay

The Best Shops

TAJMAHAL DUTY FREE STORES
Half Moon Village (☎ 876-953-9237)
34 City Centre Building (☎ 876-952-2291)

The Tajmahal Shopping Center, located in Ocho Rios, has expanded its operations and now has shops in Montego Bay. These shops feature Swarovski crystal, Fendi leather, and David

Yurman jewelry, among many other tempting products.

CASA DE ORO
36 City Centre, ☎ 876-952-3502;
Half Moon Village, ☎ 876-953-9755

Mikimoto pearls, Fendi leather, Cartier leather, Tag Heuer watches, Tiffany watches and jewelry, Rado watches, and an extensive perfume center are found in these well-known shops.

CHULANI
City Centre Boulevard, ☎ 876-952-2158;
Sangster International Airport, ☎ 876-952-2377

This large duty-free shop offers just about everything: perfumes, Anne Klein, Givenchy, fine jewelry, Cross pens and Armani.

THE FRENCH SHOP
Casa Montego Arcade
Gloucester Avenue
☎ 876-952-2991

Carrera y Carrera, Audemars Piguet, Swatch and Citizen watches, Fendi leather and Lladro collectibles.

Fine Jewelry

BIJOUX JEWELERS
57 St. James St., City Centre Bldg., ☎ 876-952-2630;
Sangster International Airport, ☎ 876-952-0255

The largest selection is found in Bijoux's City Centre store.

All locations of this well-known jeweler offer an array of tempting goods: Breitling watches, Raymond Weil watches, Swarovski crystal, Baccarat crystal, Hummel figurines, Fendi leather and more. There are two outlets at the airport.

Watches

BIJOUX JEWELERS
57 St. James St., City Centre Bldg., ☎ 876-952-2630; Sangster International Airport, ☎ 876-952-0255

Breitling and Raymond Weil watches are featured in this shop.

CASA DE ORO
Half Moon Village, ☎ 876-953-9755; 36 City Centre, ☎ 876-952-3502

Watches from Tissot, Tag Heuer, Tiffany and Rado.

TROPICANA JEWELERS
Half Moon Village, ☎ 876-953-2099; 44-44 City Centre Mall, ☎ 876-952-6982

Look for Piaget watches as well as watches by Chaumet, Gucci and Bulgari in this high-end shop with two locations.

THE ROYAL SHOP
38 City Centre Bldg., ☎ 876-853-2254; 5 Cruise Ship Terminal, ☎ 876-979-8438

Watches by makers such as Corum, Concord, Omega, Piaget and Movado are for sale here.

SWISS STORES
Half Moon Village, ☎ 876-953-2520; Montego Bay Shopping Centre, ☎ 876-952-4274

These fine stores are official Rolex distributors.

Montego Bay

GRANDE TEMPTATIONS
Trelawny Hotel
☎ 876-954-2671

Shop for watches by Seiko and Citizen in this hotel store.

China, Crystal & Figurines

BIJOUX JEWELERS
57 St. James St.
City Centre Bldg.
☎ 876-952-2630

You'll find a good selection of Swarovski crystal, including jewelry, at this shop. Lladro collectible figures are also sold here, as well as Baccarat crystal and Hummel figurines.

GRANDE TEMPTATIONS
Trelawny Hotel
☎ 876-954-2671

Collectibles such as Swarovski crystals, Lladro figurines and Armani figurines are featured here.

Fashion Boutiques

OCCHI VERDI BY VENEZIA
Half Moon Shopping Centre
☎ 876-953-3850

This fashionable boutique carries Italian high fashion, including swimsuits, menswear and dresses.

Local Crafts

CRAFT MARKET
Harbor Avenue

Many travelers avoid the market because of the high-pressure sales, but we have found it delightful. A friendly "good morning," abstaining from photos until a purchase (no matter how small) is made, and general good manners will go far with the salespeople. After shopping, take a break with a soft drink or "sky juice" (like our snow cone, but more liquid) sold from pushcarts beneath the shade trees. Some smaller items available at the market include straw baskets ($3), tiny straw purses ($4), friendship bracelets in rasta colors ($1), coffee bean necklaces ($2) and bamboo bangles ($4).

One cheerful vendor gave us a small basket as a gift.

Montego Bay

Gifts & Souvenirs

NICOLE'S FANTASY ARCADE
Gloucester Avenue
☎ 876-952-3746

This souvenir shop offers t-shirts, coffee, cigars, reggae recordings, casual wear, beach towels, local rums and inexpensive jewelry.

Nicole's also sells phone cards.

◎ TIP

For free pickup from a local hotel, give Nicole's store a call.

REGGAE STYLE
Half Moon Shopping Centre
No phone

Reggae Style is a great place for gifts and souvenirs with an island feel.

This store is one of our favorites in Mo Bay. You can buy Blue Mountain coffee candles ($15), locally-made jewelry, Wassi Art ceramics and island-themed clothing at very reasonable prices.

Art Galleries

LESTER ART GALLERY
Reading
☎ 876-952-1387

This gallery features the work of the late Polish sea captain Michael Leszczynski. Leszczynski was especially known for his Jamaica works. The gallery is located in a home he built in the 1950s. If you'll be visiting the Rocklands Feeding Station, this art gallery is located nearby.

⭐ **DID YOU KNOW?**

The name "Leszczynski" was Anglicized to Lester.

After Dark

Much of the nightlife in Montego Bay takes place in the resorts and along the "Hip Strip," the entertainment area of Gloucester Avenue.

Casino

CORAL CLIFF CASINO
Gloucester Avenue
☎ 876-952-4130

You'll find slot machines in some of the larger resorts on the island, but the most extensive gambling site is at the Coral Cliff Casino on the Hip Strip. You can't miss the casino – just look for the flashing neon lights. Only slot machine gambling is found here, but jackpots do get quite large.

Montego Bay

Discos

PLANET X
Half Moon Shopping Centre
☎ 876-953-3840

The black and white decor of the Half Moon Resort is carried out in this disco as well. Located in the shopping village, Planet Xaymaka, or Planet X, features all types of dance tunes and plenty of reggae. There is a cover charge which includes one drink.

On Sunday nights Planet X features oldies.

Theater

MONTEGO BAY LITTLE THEATRE
Fairfield Hotel
☎ 876-953-9573

This local theatrical group produces a variety of shows. Call for show days (shows always start at 8); admission is a very reasonable J$250.

Montego Bay A-Z

American Consulate

US Consular Agency
Gloucester Avenue
☎ 876-952-0160

Babysitting

Check with your hotel for babysitting services. Many offer it for as little as US$3 per hour.

Banks

Bank of Nova Scotia
Sam Sharpe Square
☎ 876-952-4440

Citizens Bank
Montego Bay Shopping Centre
Howard Cooke Boulevard, Montego Bay
☎ 876-952-4873

Currency Exchange

You can exchange US dollars into local currency at the larger hotels (at a rate usually slightly less favorable than the bank rate) or at:

Cambioman
8 Market Street, ☎ 876-940-0691

Grand Central Cambio
13 Barnett Street
☎ 876-979-9233

Joseph Heath Cambio
Overton Plaza
☎ 876-952-4404

Dentist

Union Dental Centre
Half Moon Shopping Village
☎ 876-953-9722

Emergency Phone Numbers

Ambulance 110
Police. 119
Fire 110

Hospital

Mo Bay Hope
Half Moon Resort
☎ 876-853-3981

This 24-hour medical diagnostic center is at the Half Moon Resort. It includes a dialysis center.

Optical Services

Imperial Optical
2 Corner Lane
☎ 876-952-3203

Broadbend Jamaica Ltd.
Optometrists and Opticians
25 James Street
☎ 876-940-3490

Pharmacies

You'll find many name-brand pharmaceutical items from home (albeit at somewhat higher prices) at pharmacies island-wide, including these ones in Mo Bay:

Fontana Pharmacy
Montego Bay Shopping Centre
☎ 876-952-3888

Hilton's Pharmacy
27 St. James Street
☎876-952-2455

Cornwall Pharmacy
19 Orange Street
☎ 876-979-2330

Overton Pharmacy
18 Overton Plaza
☎ 876-952-2467

Photo Labs

Several labs offer one-hour processing, including:

Pugh's Colour Lab and Photo Studio
3 St. James Street
☎ 876-979-2234

Photo Express
City Centre
☎ 876-952-3120

Ventura Photo and Video
Half Moon Village
☎ 876-953-9685

Ocho Rios

Introduction

Ocho Rios is the garden center of Jamaica and its lushest area is **Dunn's River Falls**. This spectacular waterfall, the area's top attraction, is a series of falls that cascade from the mountains to the sea. Here, you don't just view the falls, but may actually climb up them. Led by a sure-footed Jamaican guide (who wears everyone's cameras slung around his neck), groups work their way up the falls hand-in-hand like a human daisy chain.

West of Ocho Rios in the town of Oracabessa, 007 fans can visit the **James Bond Beach**. Located near Ian Fleming's former home, Goldeneye, the beach has plenty of options for a day of activity: Waverunners, helicopter tours and horseback rides, as well as beach bar and grill.

★ DID YOU KNOW?

The town of Ocho Rios is often known by the nickname "Ochi."

SEVEN-DAY OCHO RIOS & PORT ANTONIO ITINERARY	
Day One	Head to Ocho Rios and enjoy the beach.
Day Two	Take a taxi over to Dunn's River Falls. Hire a guide to lead you up the falls. After your climb, have your taxi driver take you through Fern Gully to see the beautiful ferns.
Day Three	Head into Ocho Rios for some shopping and a visit to the crafts markets. That afternoon, visit Coyaba for a look at Jamaica's history and local plants.
Day Four	Take a day trip to Port Antonio. Stop by the Blue Lagoon for some swimming in the morning; take a raft trip down the Rio Grande that afternoon.
Day Five	Take a tour of Firefly, then spend the afternoon on the beach.
Day Six	Take a tour of the Blue Mountains, home of some of the world's best coffee.
Day Seven	Spend your last day on the beach.

Getting Around

Car & Jeep Rentals

Most travelers rent vehicles in Montego Bay or Kingston, but there are some car rental agencies in Ocho Rios.

OCHO RIOS CAR RENTAL AGENCIES	
Bargain Rent-A-Car	☎ 876-974-5298 (Pineapple Place)
Island Car Rentals	☎ 876-974-2666 (Carib Arcade, Main St.)

Taxis

Taxis are the most popular method of transportation for travelers, and can be caught at any hotel, the airports, and in most shopping areas. If you need to call for a taxi, contact the official carrier: Jamaica Union of Travelers Association or **JUTA** (☎ 876-974-2292 in Ocho Rios).

TIP

Be careful to use only licensed taxis; these have a red license plate that indicates the taxi as a Public Passenger Vehicle (PPV).

Taxi rates vary, but the charge is by car, not by the number of passengers. If you accept a driver's offer of his services as a tour guide, be sure to agree on a price before the vehicle is put into gear.

Fares average about US$5-7 for 10 miles.

Not all cabs are metered, so agree on a price before entering the taxi.

Ocho Rios

Bus Service

Bus travel is popular among Jamaicans, but buses (often minibuses) can be crowded and slow. Buses will stop anywhere along the route to pick up passen-

The buses are generally not air-conditioned.

gers. To catch one, stand by the side of the road with your arm outstretched; pat down with your hand when you see an oncoming bus. Bus fare is very inexpensive – about US$1 for 30-40 miles.

Ocho Rios Tours

BLUE MOUNTAIN BICYCLE TOURS LTD.
Main Street, Ocho Rios
☎ 876-974-7075 or 974-7492, fax 876-974-0635

These downhill tours have been featured in many magazines and include brunch, lunch, refreshments and all bike equipment. The tours cover 18 downhill miles through the Blue Mountains and the tropical rain forest.

SAFARI TOURS
Mammee Bay
☎ 876-972-2639 or 876-919-7900
E-mail: Safari@toj.com
www.jamaica-irie.com/safari

This tour company offers several unique tours. See page 58 in the Montego Bay chapter for full details.

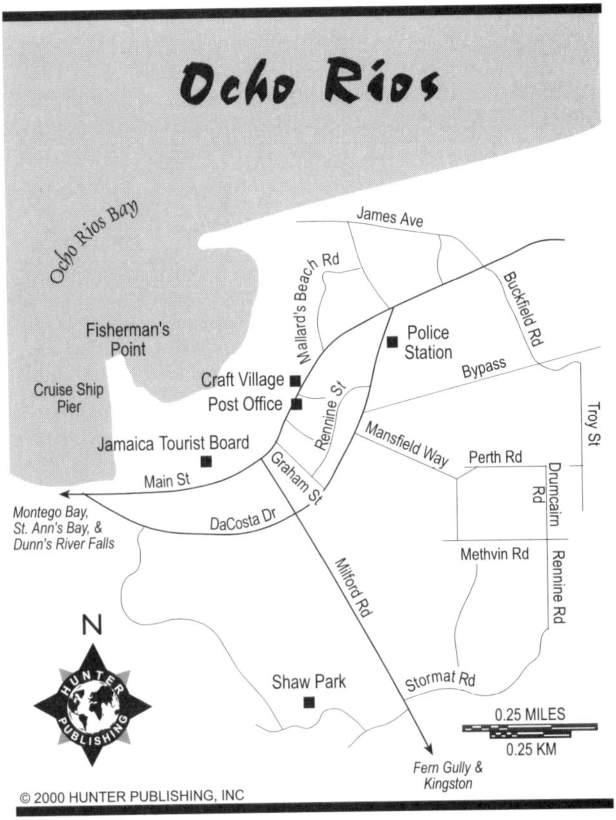

Ocho Rios

Ocho Rios Bay

James Ave

Buckfield Rd

Mallard's Beach Rd

Fisherman's
Point

Police
Station

Bypass

Cruise Ship
Pier

Craft Village ■
Post Office ■

Rennine St

Troy St

Jamaica Tourist Board ■

Mansfield Way

Perth Rd

Main St

Graham St

Drumcairn Rd

*Montego Bay,
St. Ann's Bay, &
Dunn's River Falls*

DaCosta Dr

Methvin Rd

Rennine Rd

Milford Rd

N

Shaw Park ■

Stormat Rd

0.25 MILES

0.25 KM

*Fern Gully &
Kingston*

© 2000 HUNTER PUBLISHING, INC

Ocho Rios

Orientation

Ocho Rios sits on the north coast of Jamaica. The main road, called the **North Coast Highway** or **A3** along this stretch, slices through the city, following the coastline. On the western side of Ocho Rios lies its most famous attraction: **Dunn's River Falls**. These spectacular

falls spill from the hills to the sea, and tourists enjoy hiking up the cascade, hand in hand. This entire stretch of road is lined with stony bluffs. Between the hills and the sea there is just enough room for a road and a strip of beach.

As you approach the city from the western end, driving from Montego Bay, you'll first see the cruise ship terminal. From here, you'll be moving into the town itself. The North Coast Highway becomes **DaCosta Drive**; off that and parallel runs **Main Street**, where many of the shops and the crafts market are located. The main road continues east through town toward the large resorts, most of which lie to the east of the city.

South of Ocho Rios are the hills that make this region so beautiful. **Shaw Park Gardens** and **Coyaba River Garden and Museum**, as well as the beautiful **Enchanted Garden Resort** are situated high in these green hills off Milford Road, the southern exit from town. Milford Road also travels through one of the island's most striking areas – **Fern Gully** – a tunnel of greenery.

Best Places to Stay

Money Matters

For accommodations, our price scale is designed to give you a ballpark figure for a typical stay during peak season. We've based these estimates on high season (December

15-April 15) for a standard room for two persons. These prices do not take into account options such as meal plans, dive packages, etc.

Accommodations Price Scale

Prices are given in US dollars.

Deluxe. . . . . $300+
Expensive . . . . $200-$300
Moderate . . . . $100-$200
Inexpensive. . . . . Under $100

Resorts

BOSCOBEL BEACH
East of Ocho Rios at Oracabessa
☎ 876-975-7330, fax 876-975-7370
Reservations: ☎ 800-GO-SUPER
www.superclubs.com
Deluxe (All-inclusive)

Ocho Rios

This SuperClubs resort is an excellent destination for families. Starting with the carousel horses and children's music that greet arrivals at the entrance, everything is kid-friendly at this property. Three types of rooms are offered – lanai (smallest), junior suite (with a step-down living room/kids' sleeping area with two twin beds/ couches) and two-story junior suites. The kids' program accommodates all age groups from toddlers to teens and entertains with arts and crafts, swimming, games and more. An adults-only section offers a piano bar, Italian restaurant, hot tub and pool.

Boscobel is a great choice for families!

CIBONEY
Main Street
☎ 876-974-1027, fax 876-974-7148
Reservations: ☎ 800-333-3333
www.ciboney.com
Expensive (All-inclusive)

You can rent a rooms in the great house at Ciboney.

This Radisson property is noted for its villa suites with private plunge pools. The feel of Ciboney is much different from other resorts in this area, with the atmosphere of a small subdivision, a place with street signs and roads. The 226 villas are scattered throughout the hillside and each has a pool just steps away. Transport from the main house to the 226 villas is available anytime. Ciboney offers 14 honeymoon suites with sunken baths, kitchen and living room. Each villa also comes with maid service. There's a weekly nature walk around the property, with guides pointing out lemons, limes, coconuts, guavas, mangos and other tropical fruits that are tended by 50 gardeners on staff.

COUPLES OCHO RIOS
North Coast Highway, east of Ocho Rios
☎ 876-975-4271, fax 876-975-4439
Reservations: ☎ 800-268-7537
www.couples.com
Expensive (All-inclusive)

As its name suggests, this resort is for couples only. This immensely popular all-inclusive makes vacation fun easy. It is also admirable for its promotion of off-property attractions, to which free excursions are offered. Travelers can enjoy trips to Dunn's River Falls, a day of shopping in Ocho Rios, or a sunset cruise as part of the all-inclusive offerings.

Couples has a large white sand beach with a full menu of watersports. If you want an all-over tan, a boat will carry you out to a small island specially set aside for nude sunbathing where you can enjoy plenty of sun as well as a dip in the pool and a swim-up bar.

ENCHANTED GARDEN
Eden Bower Road
☎ 876-974-1400, fax 876-974-5823
Reservations: ☎ 800-554-2008
Expensive (All-inclusive)

This romantic resort is best known for its tropical gardens and waterfalls. It is located on the hillside, with the beach just a short shuttle ride away. There are 113 rooms and five restaurants here. Facilities include tennis, a fitness center, yoga, Tai Chi, bird feeding, non-motorized watersports, and more.

The Enchanted Garden offers one-hour tours of the gardens & waterfalls.

GRAND LIDO SANS SOUCI
North Coast Highway, 2 miles east of Ocho Rios
☎ 876-974-2353, fax 876-974-2544
Reservations: ☎ 800-467-8737
www.superclubs.com
Expensive (All-inclusive)

Grand Lido Sans Souci, one of the SuperClubs chain, is ultra luxurious – the place to go for relaxation and first-class pampering. The adults-only (16 and over) resort is built on a hillside with rooms that wind from the public areas down to the beach below. There are two beaches, one of which is for *au naturel* sunbathing.

A stay here includes complimentary services at Charlie's Spa, located by a natural spring. You

Ocho Rios

While you're at the spa, keep an eye out for Charlie, the sea turtle who lives in the spring's cave.

Day and night passes for Grand Lido can be purchased by non-guests.

can have a massage, manicure, pedicure, reflexology, body scrub and facial.

Recently, the 146-suite resort added 36 one-bedroom Jacuzzi suites as well as a new freeform pool, tennis courts, a jogging track, volleyball court and an expanded games room. Your all-inclusive fee offers unlimited golf at Breezes Golf & Beach Resort, 24-hour room service, watersports and meeting facilities for up 80 participants theater-style.

RENAISSANCE JAMAICA GRANDE RESORT
Main Street
☎ 876-974-2201, fax 876-974-5378
Reservations: ☎ 800-HOTELS1
www.renaissancehotel.com
Moderate to Expensive

Jamaica Grande has a supervised children's program and is a good option for families traveling with children.

This large, sprawling hotel has the largest meeting space in Ocho Rios, and hosts many meetings and conventions. Many conventioneers bring along spouses and children, who find plenty of activity. But there are plenty of reasons to stay at Jamaica Grande even if you're on your own. We stayed here recently and enjoyed a beautiful seaside room.

Downtown Ocho Rios is just a short walk away. A protected beach offers calm, quiet waters for an afternoon swim. The swim-up bar in the pool sits beneath a 26-foot replica of Dunn's River Falls.

The resort features two towers of rooms, but our choice would be the cabana rooms, located right on the beach. Lower floor rooms step right out onto the sand.

SANDALS DUNN'S RIVER
North Coast Highway
☎ 876-972-1610, fax 876-972-1611
Reservations: ☎ 800-SANDALS
www.sandals.com
Expensive (All-inclusive)

Sandals' spa treatments are available at an à la carte price and are not part of the all-inclusive package.

This massive Sandals is custom-made for people who enjoy fun in the form of organized activity and watersports. A new spa here features a full menu of treatments, including reflexology, body scrubs and aromatherapy. It's located in a newly renovated fitness center (an open-air beauty that would inspire anyone to pump a little iron) and includes hot and cold plunge pools and private treatment rooms in a luxurious atmosphere.

Sandals Dunn's River has lots of activities!

SANDALS OCHO RIOS
North Coast Highway
☎ 876-974-5691, fax 876-974-5700
Reservations: ☎ 800-SANDALS
www.sandals.com
Expensive (All-inclusive)

Just down the road from Sandals Dunn's River, Sandals Ocho Rios is one of the most romantic resorts in the chain, located on lavishly planted grounds that bloom with birds of paradise and buzz with the sound of hummingbirds.

Ocho Rios

★ **DID YOU KNOW?**

Sandals' founder Butch Stewart grew up on these grounds; the building used for the piano bar was his grandparents' home.

Sandals Ocho Rios enjoys a beautiful setting.

Guests at Sandals Ocho Rios enjoy the "Stay at One, Dine at Six" policy and can take meals at the other Sandals properties. A reservation desk at Sandals Ocho Rios arranges reservations for meals at other properties; a free shuttle to Sandals Dunn's River makes dining at that nearby property easy.

Hotels

COMFORT SUITES CRANE RIDGE
17 DaCosta Drive
☎ 876-974-8050, fax 876-974-8070
Inexpensive to Moderate

Comfort Suites is part of Choice Hotels International.

This all-suite hotel is perched high on a hill overlooking Ocho Rios. The recent construction offers 71 one- and two-bedroom suites with balconies, air-conditioning, kitchenettes, satellite TV, telephones, fold-out sofas; two-bedroom suites also have Jacuzzi tubs. A restaurant is on property.

JAMAICA INN
Two miles east of Ocho Rios,
North Coast Highway
☎ 876-974-2514, fax 876-974-2449
Reservations: ☎ 800-837-4670
www.jamaicainn.com
Expensive to Deluxe

This classic Caribbean inn with 45 suites has drawn visitors such as model Kate Moss, Phil Donahue, Marlo Thomas and actor Albert Finney. Each suite has a beach view, private verandah and antique furnishings. The inn is also home to a noted restaurant.

PLANTATION INN
Main Street
☎ 876-974-5601, fax 876-974-5912
Reservations: ☎ 800-752-6824
Expensive (All-inclusive optional)

This 63-room hideaway, styled like an old plantation mansion, was used in the filming of *Prelude to a Kiss*, starring Meg Ryan and Alec Baldwin. The property offers plenty of activities. An all-inclusive plan is available.

SHAW PARK BEACH HOTEL
Cutlass Bay
☎ 876-974-2552, fax 876-974-5042
Reservations: ☎ 800-377-1126
www.shawpark.com
Expensive

This low-rise hotel is set on a long stretch of white beach. It offers 33 standard guest rooms with shower only, 60 superior (with both a shower and tub) and 13 suites. Regardless of category, every room has a balcony or terrace overlooking the sea.

Amenities include deep-sea fishing, sailing, windsurfing, scuba diving, aerobics, tennis and a children's play area.

Ocho Rios

Intimate Inns

GOLDENEYE
Oracabessa, St. Mary
☎ 876-975-3354, fax 876-975-3679
Reservations: ☎ 800-OUTPOST
www.islandlife.com
Deluxe

If you've won the lottery and you're wondering where to stay on your next visit to Jamaica, this might just be the place. Located eight minutes from Oracabessa (15 minutes from Ochi), Goldeneye is a one-of-a-kind getaway.

James Bond buffs, here's your chance to feel like Ian Fleming himself: Goldeneye was the author's home.

The Goldeneye house itself is available for rent at $5,000 per day for up to six guests. The Ian Fleming Villa, a three-bedroom accommodation, has a garden dining area, private beach and full-time staff to whip up meals. A private TV room features a big screen TV, satellite programming, VCR, bar and more.

Another option is Goldeneye Village, a flexible configuration of cottages (eight total bedrooms) that may be rented as individual units or as a group. Each has indoor and outdoor dining facilities, kitchen, private beach access and entertainment/TV room. These units are newly built and decorated with local artwork and fabrics.

Each of these guests planted a tree on the grounds at Goldeneye. Trees are marked with small plaques.

Seeing Stars

Goldeneye has seen many celebrities. During Fleming's lifetime, the writer played host to Noel Coward, Errol Flynn and Elizabeth Taylor. Now, as part of Chris Blackwell's empire, the property's stellar guest list has included Martha Stewart, Jim Carrey, Christy Turlington, Quincy Jones, Harry Belafonte and Naomi Campbell.

Best Places to Eat

All-Inclusive Dining

If you see a restaurant designated as "all-inclusive" in the price listing, this is a restaurant located on an all-inclusive resort. Guests at the resort can dine there as part of their package. But what if you're not staying there?

Have no fear. Most all-inclusives sell both day and evening passes which allow non-guests to come on-property and enjoy the amenities. Everyone comes out a winner. You get to try a new restaurant and the resort tempts you to book your next vacation with them.

Money Matters

For dining, we've set up a price scale based on a three-course dinner including appetizer or soup, an entrée, dessert and coffee. Cocktails and wine are extra.

Dining Price Scale

Prices are per person in US dollars.

Expensive. . . . . $40+ per person
Moderate . . . . $25-$40
Inexpensive. . . . . Under $25

Ocho Rios

Recommended Restaurants

ALMOND TREE

83 Main Street
☎ 876-974-2813
Moderate to Expensive

Reservations are required at the Almond Tree.

The menu at this popular eatery reflects both Jamaican and continental tastes. Live music entertains diners three times weekly.

BAYSIDE

Couples Ocho Rios
North Coast Highway, east of Ocho Rios
☎ 876-975-4271
All-inclusive

Bayside is the perfect spot for a dinner right by the water's edge. As its name suggests, this open-air eatery is located right on the bay, tucked beneath roofs.

Specialties of the house are Italian, with a wide selection of pasta sauces from which to choose. The restaurant is open for dinner only from 6:30 to 9:30 pm.

⊚ TIP

If you are not a guest at Couples Ocho Rios, you can purchase an evening pass which includes drinks during your stay, the evening's meal (including tips) and the nightly show.

CALABASH

Couples Ocho Rios
North Coast Highway, east of Ocho Rios
☎ 876-975-4271
All-inclusive

This Jamaican restaurant serves dinner nightly (except Wednesday and Saturday). Each of the dishes reflects the rich cuisine of the island, starting with appetizers such as May Pen mushroom pie and Marley marinade, scallops and crabcakes mixed with virgin olive oil, balsamic vinegar and herbs. Entrées include mahi-mahi with grilled pineapple and curried tomato vinaigrette, Kingston Kiev chicken breast stuffed with herbed garlic butter, and baked christophines (cho-cho) with vegetable spaghetti and red pepper sauce. There's also jerked chicken, jerked pork, red snapper escovitch and peppered steak.

CASANOVA

Grand Lido Sans Souci
North Coast Highway, 2 miles east of Ocho Rios
☎ 876-974-2353
All-inclusive

This restaurant (open nightly except Friday) serves gourmet French cuisine in a casually elegant setting.

Casanova menu selections include nut-crushed snapper, fillet of salmon served with saffron and champagne sauce, baked sea trout topped with basil hollandaise sauce, pot-roasted guinea fowl with port game sauce, seared duck stuffed with goose liver and nuts, jerk chicken roulade stuffed with callaloo and tournedos of pork.

Ocho Rios

Jackets are required and reservations are recommended two days in advance.

DRAGONS
Renaissance Jamaica Grande
Main Street, Ocho Rios
☎ 876-974-2201
Moderate

If you're ready for a break from Caribbean dishes, try some authentic Cantonese and Szechwan cooking. Located in the South Tower Lobby adjoining the Dragons Lounge, this delightful restaurant is open 6 to 11 pm for dinner.

Dragons menu selections include: sweet and sour pork, Szechwan-style chicken and nuts, chow mein, duck in plum sauce, lemon fish and fried rice.

EVITA'S
Mantalent Inn, Eden Bower Road
☎ 876-974-2333
Inexpensive to Moderate

Evita's has been featured in Gourmet, Bon Appetit, and other publications.

This longtime favorite is patronized by travelers and locals alike for good Italian fare. Perched high over the city in a house more than a century old, Evita's is especially noted for its numerous pasta and seafood dishes.

Evita's has a long and illustrious history. Operated by Eva Myers from Venice, Italy, the restaurant has attracted many well-known guests, including Michael Bolton, Phil Donahue, Marlo Thomas, Meg Ryan, Alec Baldwin, Chris Blackwell, Princess Margaret, Naomi Campbell, Kate Moss, Christy Turlington, Keith Richards and the Rolling Stones, Ali Campbell, UB40 and more.

Menu selections include: homemade fettuccine with meat sauce, fettucine Alfredo, red snapper fillet stuffed with crabmeat and jumbo shrimp sautéed in garlic butter, white wine and tomatoes.

THE INTERNATIONAL ROOM
Sandals Dunn's River
North Coast Highway
☎ 876-972-1610
All-inclusive

This elegant indoor restaurant serves up gourmet cuisine. Try the seared fillet of salmon with key lime, beurre blanc and saffron vegetable risotto. It's delicious. Other selections include chargrilled reef snapper dusted with Jamaican allspice and served with papaya ginger salsa and grilled plantains and fresh shrimp sautéed in garlic butter with fennel cream sauce.

Long pants and collared shirts are required for men at the International Room.

Ocho Rios

JAMAICA INN
Two miles east of Ocho Rios,
North Coast Highway
☎ 876-974-2514, fax 876-974-2449
Expensive

Chef Wilbert Matheson serves up varied fare in this al fresco restaurant. Jacket and tie are required after 7 pm in all but the summer season. No children under age 14 are permitted to dine here, as the restaurant strives for an elegant atmosphere. Reservations are required.

The Jamaica Inn has been featured in Gourmet *and* Food and Wine *magazines.*

Some of the most tempting entrées are grilled beef tenderloin topped with chicken liver compote, poached yellowtail tuna with steamed mussels and tomato concasse and porkloin with a pineapple and honey glaze.

L'ALLEGRO
Renaissance Jamaica Grande
Main Street
Moderate to Expensive

L'Allegro offers a menu especially for children.

This restaurant, with both indoor and open-air seating, offers fine Northern Italian cuisine, including pizzas made in a Tuscan wood-burning brick oven. Selections include: quattro stagioni pizza with blue cheese, tuna, artichoke and bacon; jerked spiced chicken, yam and jerked tomato sauce with mozzarella cheese pizza. Located in the South Tower of the resort, this restaurant offers an extensive wine list.

LE GOURMET RESTAURANT
Couples Ocho Rios
North Coast Highway, east of Ocho Rios
☎ 876-975-4271
All-inclusive

Reservations are required at Le Gourmet.

This elegant French restaurant offers two seatings at 6:30 and 8:30 nightly, except Wednesdays. Mouth-watering dishes include: Cajun-style blackened snapper fillet and jambalya rice; sautéed veal medallion with roasted garlic; and steamed grouper stuffed with crab and spinach on a spicy butter sauce, topped with crisp grated potato garnish.

MANOR RESTAURANT
Ciboney, Main Street
☎ 876-974-1027
All-inclusive

Reservations are required at the Manor.

Jamaican dishes prepared with a gourmet flair are the order of the day at this elegant eatery.

MICHELLE'S
Sandals Ocho Rios
North Coast Highway
☎ 876-974-5691
All-inclusive

This couples-only restaurant serves Northern Italian fare. Try the pan-fried swordfish, filet of snapper and shrimp baked in a paper pouch or the beef medallions in a tomato and herb sauce with creamy polenta.

Long pants & collared shirts are required at Michelle's, as are reservations.

OCHO RIOS VILLAGE JERK CENTRE
DaCosta Drive
☎ 876-974-2549
Inexpensive to Moderate

The Jerk Centre has a casual atmosphere.

This open-air eatery looks like an all-American hamburger joint with its striped canopy and casual atmosphere, but take a whiff of that smoky jerk and you'll know this is no burger bar. Jamaican jerk is the star of the day here; try the pork, chicken or fish.

Ocho Rios

ORCHIDS
Ciboney
Main Street
☎ 876-974-1027
All-inclusive

This resort is noted not only for its villa suites with private plunge pools but also for its cuisine. The signature restaurant is Orchids, featuring nutritional gourmet cuisine developed in conjunction with the Culinary Institute of America.

We recommend that you make reservations at Orchids.

PLANTATION INN
Main Street
☎ 876-974-5601
Expensive

Make reservations for a meal at the Plantation Inn.

This elegant restaurant has been a favorite with Jamaica vacationers for over four decades. Guests can start their day with breakfast served right on their oceanview balcony, complete with starched linens and silver service. Or they can opt for breakfast in the main dining room with local specialties such as ackee and codfish, liver and bananas, pan-fried fish, or eggs, pancakes and freshly-baked breads.

RISTORANTE D'AMORE
Sandals Dunn's River
North Coast Highway
☎ 876-972-1610
All-inclusive

Long pants & collared shirts are required at the Ristorante D'Amore.

Italian fare is the order of the day at this couples-only restaurant, with two courses as well as delicious desserts such as tiramisu or chocolate and amaretto cheesecake. Main dishes include: grilled snapper filet; chicken breast simmered in tomatoes; veal cutlets with fontina and prosciutto sautéed in butter and wine; and pork medallions sautéed in olive oil with capers, garlic, and lime juice.

THE RUINS
DaCosta Drive
☎ 876-974-2442
Moderate to Expensive

This restaurant is perched right beside a waterfall, its tables at the base of a 40-foot cascade. The menu here is diverse, with Oriental specialties such as lotus lily lobster and Far Eastern chicken, Jamaican specials, and even vegetarian dishes.

The History of the Ruins

The site of the restaurant has an interesting history. In 1831, Englishman Robert Rutherford built a sugar factory near these falls, using their energy to grind the cane. Allegedly, he married a local girl named Rose Dale and they moved into a great house near the falls. Later, while Rutherford was in England on business, Rose fell in love with one of the plantation's overseers. When her husband returned home, he learned of his wife's indiscretions and began spending time with Annie Palmer, better known as the White Witch of Rose Hall (see page 96) in Montego Bay. One night, after finding his wife with her lover, he took Rose and the lover to a cave between the falls, chained the couple to the walls, and sealed the cave with a boulder. Later Rutherford married Annie Palmer and the plantation became, literally, ruins.

The Ruins is a wonderfully romantic spot for lunch or dinner.

Ocho Rios

SULTAN'S TABLE
The Enchanted Garden
Eden Bower Road
☎ 876-974-1400
All-inclusive

This fine dining restaurant serves up Middle Eastern delights from Morocco, Lebanon, Israel, Algeria and Turkey. The theme is carried out in

Reservations are required at the Sultan's Table.

the resplendent decor of this eatery, which features rich Turkish rugs, ornate brass screens and hand-carved ornaments.

Offerings include stuffed peppers with beef and cous cous; slow-cooked chicken with chick peas; and snapper filet with tahini-yogurt sauce.

TEMPLES
The Enchanted Garden
Eden Bower Road
☎ 876-974-1400
All-inclusive

Make advance reservations for an evening at Temples.

This elegant Asian restaurant serves Thai, Japanese, Indonesian and regional Chinese cuisine. Couples dine on cushions in a rich Asian atmosphere that features Oriental rugs, bronze fish and hanging chandeliers.

Entrée selections include: curry beef, chicken and bamboo shoots with lemon grass sauce; Thai seafood fried rice; and spicy Bangkok stir-fried vegetables with ginger-chili sauce.

TEPPANYAKI
Sandals Dunn's River
North Coast Highway
☎ 876-972-1610
All-inclusive

Long pants & collared shirts are required at Teppanyaki, as are reservations.

Asian cuisine prepared at table-side by Teppanyaki chefs draw diners to this fun restaurant. A popular choice here is the Emperor's Feast, a selection of dishes such as oyster-flavored tiger shrimp, and glazed tuna teryaki. End the evening with a sweet taste of Asia such as lychee custard with an essence of orange blossom.

TOSCANINI ITALIAN
RESTAURANT AT HARMONY HALL
Tower Isle
☎ 876-975 4785
Expensive

When you're ready to take a break from shopping at Harmony Hall (see *Shop Till You Drop* for more details on that diversion), refuel with a stop at this authentic Italian restaurant open for lunch and dinner. The menu offers many classic Italian dishes supplemented by ever-changing specials, dependent upon available fresh produce. The carefully selected wine list features vintages from around the world, while the fully stocked bar caters to all tastes. Toscanini is popular with visitors and local residents. Its delightful setting makes it an ideal spot for lunch, light or long, and for a romantic candlelit dinner.

WINDIES
Sandals Dunn's River
North Coast Highway
☎ 876-972-1610
All-inclusive

West Indian food with a gourmet flair is served by white-gloved waiters and waitresses at this elegant restaurant for couples only. Offerings at this casually elegant restaurant include Arawak-style jerk chicken and port; aged striploin steak; red snapper fillet infused with Seville orange marmalade grilled over charcoal; and lamb steak pan roasted with wild island onions.

Ocho Rios

Dressy shorts are permitted at Windies.

Sunup To Sundown

Ocho Rios offers a wide variety of activities, from ecotourism hikes to picnicking to horseback riding. Nature lovers will love this area, which is one of Jamaica's top destinations.

Beaches

Ocho Rios is home to several beautiful beaches. The resort beaches are private and restricted to use by guests or those who have obtained day passes.

James Bond Beach is west of Ocho Rios in the town of Oracabessa in the parish of St. Mary. The beach is near Ian Fleming's home, Goldeneye, and has plenty of activities, including Waverunners, helicopter tours and horseback rides as well as beach bar and grill. Admission charged.

Nude & Topless Beaches

Guests or day pass visitors at the SuperClubs area resorts (Grand Lido Sans Souci, Grand Lido Braco) or Couples Ocho Rios have nude beaches on-site. The Couples Ocho Rios beach is especially unusual because it is located on a small offshore island that includes a swim-up bar and a pool as well as hammocks and restrooms.

Scuba Diving

Dive operators are found at most of the all-inclusive hotels, including Couples, Enchanted Gardens, both Sandals and Sans Souci.

DIVE OPERATORS	
Boscobel	☎ 876-974-2353 or 957-7330
Couples Ocho Rios	☎ 876-975-4271/2/3/4/5
Enchanted Gardens	☎ 876-972-1937
Jamaqua Dive Centre	☎ 876-973-4845
Resort Divers	☎ 876-974-5338
Reef Divers	☎ 876-973-4400
Seaworld Resorts	☎ 876-953-2250 (Cariblue Beach Hotel) ☎ 876-974-5691 (Sandals Ocho Rios)
Sandals Dunn's River	☎ 876-972-1750-972-1610
Sans Souci Lido	☎ 876-974-2353 or 957-7330

Ocho Rios

Horseback Riding

CHUKKA COVE EQUESTRIAN CENTRE
North Coast Highway
between Runaway Bay and Ocho Rios
☎ 876-972-2506, fax 876-972-0814
Open daily
Admission

Chukka Cove is well known for its world-class polo matches, but the center also offers guided horseback trips along the beach and in the mountains. They operate a very popular three-hour beach ride for beginners and experienced riders

Bring your swimsuit for the ride in the sea!

that departs daily at 9 am and 2 pm. The trip takes you through Richmond and Llandovery, two of the oldest sugar estates on the island. Shower facilities on the beach are available and free refreshments are served.

Fishing

Go out with an operator for a half-day or full day of deep-sea fishing.

FISHING OPERATORS	
Broadreach Cruises	☎ 876-974-2527
King Fisher & Sun Fisher	☎ 876-974-2726 or 974-2260
Mitzy	☎ 876-974-2527 or 957-4224
Sunfisher Ltd.	☎ 876-994-2294
Triple "B"	☎ 876-975-3273

Golf

The Sandals course offers a good view of the sea at the 10th hole.

SANDALS GOLF AND COUNTRY CLUB
☎ 876-975-0119

This course takes advantage of the verdant scenery for which Ocho Rios is known. The lovely clubhouse has an elegant restaurant and bar to enjoy after play. Par 72.

Unique Tours

HELITOURS

120 Main Street
☎ 876-974-2264, fax 876-974-2183
Admission

For the best view of Ocho Rios, consider a quick helicopter tour. We tried this once, traveling from the Couples Resort up the coast to get a bird's-eye view of Goldeneye, and it was truly an experience to remember. The operator offers three tours. The *Jamaican Showcase* lasts one hour and goes all the way to Kingston and Port Maria. The *Memories of Jamaica* tour, a half-hour ride, travels over Noel Coward's Firefly and Ian Fleming's Goldeneye. The *Ocho Rios Fun Hop*, a 15-minute trip, swings over Shaw Park Gardens, Fern Gully, Prospect Plantation and Dunn's River Falls.

PROSPECT PLANTATION TOUR

☎ 876-974-2058
Admission

If you're interested in learning about Jamaica's fruits, this is an excellent opportunity. This working farm takes visitors by tractor-drawn jitney or on horseback to view fields of bananas, cassava, sugar cane, coffee, allspice and more.

SAFARI TOURS

☎ 876-972-2639 or 919-7900, phone and fax
E-mail: Safari@toj.com
www.jamaica-irie.com-safari
Admission

One of Jamaica's most respected companies, this operator has a variety of tours ranging in price from $69 to $86. Options include a jeep safari with stops at the Lime Juice Factory and a rum distillery with a picnic lunch on the beach and a trip through the Blue Mountains to visit a coffee farmer and tour World's End, home of Sangster's liqueur factory. Bicycle tours to Dunn's River Falls, horseback riding and river tubing and shopping round out the offerings.

Sights & Attractions

COYABA RIVER GARDEN AND MUSEUM
Shaw Park Estate, Shaw Park Ridge Road
☎ 876-974-6235
Hours: 8:30 - 5 daily
Admission

Coyaba is a good stop for history & botanical buffs.

A small but nice museum starts with pre-Columbian history and follows the development of the island through the years. The real splendor of the attraction, however, lies in its beautiful gardens. Stroll past natural springs and water-falls, where small pools are filled with colorful koi and turtles.

CRANBROOK FLOWER FOREST
West of Ocho Rios at Laughlands, one mile off North Coast Highway (sign on left one mile past Chukka Cove)
Hours: 9 - 5:30 daily
☎ 876-770-8071 or 995-3097
Admission

Cranbrook is one place that should not be missed!

This beautiful park, a recent addition to Ochi's tourist offerings, is a must-see for anyone who wants to experience the lush beauty away from the crowds. This park is the private creation of Ivan Linton, who has pampered the plants of this former plantation for over two decades. Today, Linton proudly points out the bird of paradise, croton, ginger, heliconia and begonias like his dear children.

The grounds are perfect for a picnic followed by a hike alongside a shady river. The path climbs high into the hills to a waterfall paradise. The day we journeyed here, children were playing in the river as their mothers did the week's laundry in the shallow water of the river.

Other activities include bird watching, pond fishing, croquet, donkey rides and volleyball.

⊚ TIP

Wear good walking shoes for the hike at Cranbrook.

Ocho Rios

DUNN'S RIVER FALLS
DaCosta Drive
☎ 876-974-2857
Hours: 8 - 5 daily
Admission

In Ocho Rios, the most popular attraction (one that just about every cruise ship passenger and resort guest enjoys) is Dunn's River Falls. This spectacular series of falls that cascade from the mountains to the sea is actually climbable. Sure-footed Jamaican guides (who wear everyone's cameras around their necks) lead groups up the falls hand-in-hand. At the end of the climb, you'll be deposited into a hectic market for another opportunity to buy crafts, carvings and the ubiquitous t-shirts.

Be sure to tip your guide.

⚠ **WARNING**

Be prepared to get wet and have fun at Dunn's River Falls, but don't expect a quiet, private get-away. This is Jamaica for the masses, and, no matter what day of the week it is, the masses do come.

FERN GULLY
A3, south of Ocho Rios
Open daily
Free

Fern Gully is a stretch of Highway A3 that winds south from Ocho Rios. For three miles, the road is lined with lush ferns and innumerable plants; well worth a drive even if you're not headed that way.

FIREFLY
Port Maria
☎ 876-997-7201
Hours: 8:30 - 5:30 daily
Admission

Today, Firefly is kept in the same state it was when the Queen Mother came to lunch in 1965.

The historic home of playwright Noel Coward offers a nice tour. Named for the luminous insects seen in the warm evenings, this house has certainly entertained its share of luminaries from the political and entertainment worlds, including Queen Elizabeth II, Laurence Olivier, Sophia Loren, Elizabeth Taylor, Alec Guiness, Peter O'Toole and Richard Burton.

A tour of Firefly includes a look at the home, photos of the house's many celebrity guests and the grounds where Coward is now buried.

SHAW PARK BOTANICAL GARDENS
☎ 876-974-2723
Cutlass Bay
Hours: 8 - 5 daily
Admission

These beautiful 25-acre gardens are perched high above Ocho Rios with excellent views of the bay and the coast. The gardens include a stunning waterfall as well as many tropical blooms.

Shop Till You Drop

Ocho Rios is one of the best shopping areas on the island, with a full array of duty-free outlets as well as crafts markets.

Ocho Rios

Shopping Centers

TAJ MAHAL SHOPPING CENTER

This is a complex of fine duty-free shops and other stores that sell souvenir items, liquor and Blue Mountain coffee. It's easy to find – just look for the building shaped like the Taj Mahal!

SONI'S PLAZA
Main Street

Soni's Plaza, filled with duty-free shops offering good buys on jewelry, watches, perfumes, liquor and more, is a favorite with many shoppers. Many of the hotel personnel we talked with in the down-town area shopped regularly at Soni's for clothing and jewelry.

Jamaica Finds

Throughout Jamaica's resort areas, you'll find many duty-free shops devoted to the world's best perfumes, jewelry, watches, and leathers. But don't forget Jamaica's home-grown gifts during your shopping tour. Here's what to look for:

◎ **Liquors.** Jamaica makes several excellent rums. **Appleton** and **Myer's** are the best known; **Sangster's** is another top name. **Tia Maria** liqueur, a coffee-flavored delight, is another popular purchase. And there's always **Red Stripe** beer if you're watching your pennies.

You can buy Blue Mountain coffee for less at local markets.

◎ **Coffee. Blue Mountain** coffee is considered one of the finest in the world. Gift shops at the resorts and the airport sell it in small burlap gift bags for about US$1 per ounce (less than half the price found in American coffee shops).

◎ **Artwork.** Jamaican crafts are some of the best in the Caribbean. Look for **wood carvings**; lignum vitae creations are the priciest but the most beautiful.

Fine Jewelry

BIJOUX JEWELERS
Taj Mahal Shopping Centre
☎ 876-974-5446

All locations of this well-known jeweler offer an array of tempting goods: Breitling watches, Raymond Weil watches, Swarovski crystal, Baccarat crystal, Hummel figurines, Fendi leather and more.

CASA DE ORO
19 Soni's Plaza, ☎ 876-974-5392;
7 Taj Mahal Centre, ☎ 876-795-2924

Mikimoto pearls, Fendi leather, Cartier leather, Tag Heuer watches, Tiffany watches and jewelry, Rado watches, and an extensive perfume center are found in these well-known shops.

CHULANI JEWELERS
Soni's Plaza
☎ 876-974-2421

Look for fine gold and gemstone jewelry here as well as watches and fine perfumes.

MOHAN'S DUTY FREE SHOP
Taj Mahal Shopping Centre
☎ 876-974-9574

You'll also find crystal, perfumes, cigars, Cross and Parker pens and Swiss Army knives.

Mohan's claims to have over 3,000 rings in inventory!

Ocho Rios

Watches

COLORS DUTY FREE JEWELLERS
Taj Mahal Plaza, ☎ 876-974-2769;
Soni's Plaza, ☎ 876-974-9271

These stores offer a wide selection of fine jewelry –
earrings, gemstone rings, watches and bracelets –
as well as cigars.

GOLD MINE
Soni's Plaza
☎ 876-974-9267

This store features Krieger, Bulova, Swiss Military watches and fine jewelry.

THE ROYAL SHOP
1 Taj Mahal Shopping Centre, ☎ 876-974-5311;
8 Soni's Plaza, ☎ 876-795-2607

This shop offers a wide variety of duty-free goods,
including a good selection of fine jewelry.

SWISS STORES
Ocean Village Shopping Centre
Main Street
☎ 876-974-2061

This fine store sells Rolex, Swiss Army, Gucci and
many other top names.

China, Crystal & Figurines

MOHAN'S DUTY FREE SHOP
Taj Mahal Shopping Centre
☎ 876-974-9574

Mohan's sells fine crystal.

Cigars

COLORS DUTY FREE JEWELLERS
Taj Mahal Plaza
☎ 876-974-2769

Cigars from Montecristo, Cohiba, Romeo y Julieta, H. Upmann, Julianas and Partagas are stocked at this store.

Local Crafts

Ocho Rios has two craft parks, both off Main Street. The **Ocho Rios Craft Park**, opposite the Ocean Village Shopping Centre, is open 8-6, Monday through Saturday. It has 154 vendors with everything from sandals to wood carvings to straw goods. The **Olde Market Craft Shoppes** is nearby and also has plenty of handmade goods.

> ◎ **TIP**
>
> Expect to bargain for prices at both places, but do it in good fun and you'll find that the vendors are not as high-pressure as they seem.

Art Galleries

WASSI ART POTTERY WORKS
Back Street
Great Pond (east side of Ocho Rios)
☎ 876-974-5044

Ocho Rios

This shop offers a tour of its factory. Visitors learn that the pottery is made of clay from Castleton, a small town in the mountains of northeast Jamaica. The clay is made into a variety of objects – tiles, sculptures, plates, candlesticks – and sold at the store and at fine boutiques throughout Jamaica.

HARMONY HALL
☎ 876-975-4222 or 876-974-2870
Free

This excellent art gallery is one of Jamaica's best and a good place to purchase original works of art. Don't miss the Annabella boxes, souvenir boxes decorated with Jamaican art.

After Dark

Much of the late-night action in Ocho Rios takes place in the resorts and along a stretch of James Street known as the "Reggae Strip." The area is similar, although smaller in scale, to Mo Bay's Hip Strip. This Reggae Strip (located directly across from the Renaissance Jamaica Grande) comes alive every Thursday evening starting at 7 pm. At that time, the street bustles with live entertainers and booths offering local cuisine.

Discos

JAMAIC'N ME CRAZY
Renaissance Jamaica Grande
Main Street
☎ 876-974-2201

This pulsating nightclub is popular with locals and guests of the resort.

West Indies Show

LITTLE PUB
Main Street
☎ 876-974-2324

This club offers Caribbean shows several times every week; call for times and dates.

Ocho Rios A-Z

Babysitting

Many of the larger resorts offer babysitting services. Check with the concierge for recommendations.

Banks

Bank of Nova Scotia
Main Street
☎ 876-974-2081

Ocho Rios

Citizens Bank
Newlin Street
☎ 876-974-5953

Currency Exchange

Most large resorts offer currency exchange (at a rate slightly less favorable than the bank rate). You can also exchange money at:

Cambioman
19 Main Street
☎ 876-974-6715

Jamswi Cambio
135 Main Street
☎ 876-974-7114

Emergency Phone Numbers

Ambulance 110
Police 119
Fire 110

Optical Services

Broadbend Jamaica Ltd.
Optometrists and Opticians
2 Newlin Street
☎ 876-974-2193

Pharmacies

Great House Pharmacy
DaCosta Drive, ☎ 876-974-2352

The New Ocho Rios Pharmacy
New Ocho Rios Plaza, Main Street
☎ 876-974-5534

Ocho Rios Pharmacy
Ocean Village Shopping Centre
☎ 876-974-2398

Photo Labs

Pugh's Colour Lab
70 Main Street
☎ 876-974-7502

Frank Bailey's Photo Studio and Colour Lab
2 Rennie Road
☎ 876-974-2711

Nev's Studio of Photography
P&J Plaza
7 DaCosta Drive
☎ 876-974-5828

Ocho Rios

Room Tax

In lieu of a room tax, guests are charged a 15% general consumption tax. This applies throughout Jamaica.

Spas

You'll find excellent spas at **Grand Lido Sans Souci**, ☎ 876-974-2353, and **Sandals Dunn's River**, ☎ 876-972-1610.

Port Antonio

Introduction

When you've had your fill of Jamaica's bustling resorts, there's a sure antidote to the tourist scene: Port Antonio. This quiet niche on Jamaica's east end is a two-hour drive from Ocho Rios and is favored by those looking to get away from it all. Don't look for mixology classes or limbo dances here; this end of Jamaica is quiet and relaxed. Fun is usually found outdoors during the day, followed by a fine meal that evening.

The drive from Ocho Rios to Port Antonio is an attraction in itself. The distance is not that long, but budget at least two hours for the journey (without stops) because of the slow, winding roads. You might think the road is bumpy, but rest assured that it was once much worse... what you now bounce along is the new and improved road!

Potholes speckle the drive from Ochi to Port Antonio, so hang on.

Dutchies

Watch for small, wooden stands covered with shiny silver pots. These cast iron pots, called dutchies (Dutch ovens), are used in both the oven and on the stovetop to prepare soups and stews. The pots are first formed in clay then done in cast iron, often crafted by Rastafarians.

This stretch of road is also notable for its innumerable produce stands. Like a drive-through grocery, every bend brings another charming stand overflowing with picturesque displays of colorful fruits and vegetables. The offerings vary by time of year, but expect to see bunches of carrots, pineapples, coconuts, yams, bananas, plantains and the large jackfruit, an odorous fruit with a staining juice that can be sliced and served, stewed or curried.

Banana plantations, notably the massive **St. Mary Banana Estate**, stretch for miles along this road.

⚡ WARNING

Trespassers are not tolerated in the plantations. Take your photos from the roadside and tread no further.

One interesting thing to note are the "blue dresses," worn by the banana stalks. To protect the growing bananas from insects, blue plastic bags are slipped over each stalk, creating a blue and green landscape for miles.

A Star-Studded Introduction

Port Antonio first came to the attention of the travel world thanks to resident Errol Flynn. The rambunctious actor had a home on Navy Island, just off the coast of Port Antonio, and entertained many celebrities in his verdant hideaway.

In the 1950s Errol Flynn started what has become one of Jamaica's top tourist activities. Noting the banana farmers taking their produce down to market on long bamboo rafts on the Rio Grande, he one day asked for a ride. Soon, the notorious lover was floating women down the expansive river, naming one section that winds between two boulders Lovers Lane.

Before long, tourists were floating down the river two by two on rafts poled by expert raftsmen. The activity has spread to several other rivers in Jamaica, but the Rio Grande remains the largest operation of its kind.

Errol Flynn wasn't the only celebrity to grace Port Antonio. Poet Ella Willa Wilcox called this "the most exquisite spot on earth." Robin Moore came to the area to pen *The French Connection*.

An historic house here stands as a tribute to lost love. The ruins of "Folly," built by a wealthy American for a sweetheart who would not come to Port Antonio, can still be seen near the main road. Why is this home now in ruins? Sea water instead of freshwater was used in making the cement and the castle crumbled.

In more recent years, many other celebrities have frequented this site and Port Antonio has found its way into the movies.

One star-studded site is the **Blue Lagoon** (remember the Brooke Shields' movie?). The beautiful swimming hole that's been termed "bottomless" because of its uncanny blue hue is

Port Antonio

actually about 180 feet deep. Take a walk through the restaurant to see the many celebrities who have visited, their photos framed on the walls. Nearby, **Boston Beach** is the place to go on the island for jerk, slow-cooked in pits.

Getting Around

Car & Jeep Rentals

Most travelers rent cars before they arrive in Port Antonio, but there are a couple of options in town.

PORT ANTONIO CAR RENTAL AGENCIES	
Eastern Rent-A-Car	☎ 876-993-32426 Harbour St.
Waves Enterprises	☎ 876-993-32063 Boundbrook Ave.

Taxis

You won't find as many taxis here as in the main resort destinations, but they are still the most popular mode of visitor transportation.

⊙ TIP

Travel in PPV-plated vehicles (red tags), which are licensed taxi drivers. If you don't find one, hotels are happy to call one.

Taxi rates are by car, not by passenger. Fares average about US$5-7 for 10 miles. If you accept a driver's offer of his services as a tour guide, be sure to agree on a price before the vehicle is put into gear.

Few of Jamaica's taxis are metered.

Bus Service

Bus travel is popular among locals but can be crowded and slow. The buses (often minibuses) are generally not air-conditioned. Buses will stop anywhere along the route to pick up passengers. To catch one, stand by the side of the road with your arm outstretched; pat down with your hand when you see an oncoming bus. Bus fare is about US$1 for 30-40 miles.

Orientation

From the west, your first introduction to Port Antonio is the massive **Rio Grande**, which tumbles from the mountains into the sea. It is home of the longest-running tourist raft business on Jamaica.

The North Coast Road becomes West Palm Avenue as it enters town along the waterfront, an area that faces **West Harbour**. In this harbor, you'll find a five-minute ferry ride delivers you to **Navy Island**, a good place to spend the day. Navy Island is the former home of actor Errol Flynn.

Port Antonio

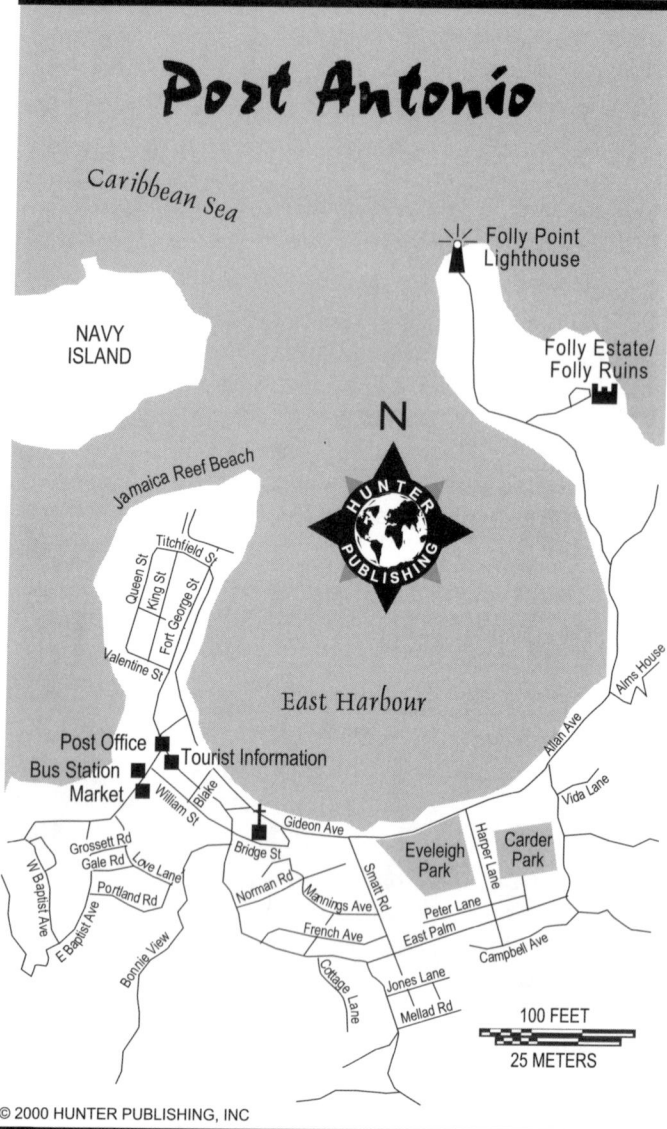

Port Antonio

Caribbean Sea

Folly Point
Lighthouse

NAVY
ISLAND

Folly Estate/
Folly Ruins

N

HUNTER PUBLISHING

Jamaica Reef Beach

Titchfield St

Queen St

King St

Fort George St

Valentine St

East Harbour

Post Office

Tourist Information

Bus Station

Market

William St

Blake

Bridge St

Gideon Ave

Allan Ave

Alms House

Vida Lane

Grossett Rd

Gale Rd

Love Lane

Norman Rd

Mannings Ave

Smeff Rd

Eveleigh
Park

Harper Lane

Carder
Park

W Baptist Ave

E Baptist Ave

Portland Rd

French Ave

East Palm

Peter Lane

Campbell Ave

Bonnie View

Cottage Lane

Jones Lane

Mellad Rd

100 FEET

25 METERS

Divided by a small peninsula, West Harbour soon gives way to East Harbour and West Palm Avenue becomes West Harbour Avenue and, finally, Allen Avenue, tracing the waterfront through town. On the end of the next peninsula stand the ruins of **Folly**.

The road continues east through the city past many of the area resorts, starting with Trident and the nearby **Trident Castle**, built by an heiress and today used by guests of Trident Resort. Farther south lies the **Blue Hole**, one of Jamaica's loveliest swimming spots and a great place to spend a lazy afternoon. Continuing south is **Boston Bay**, home of some of the best jerk chicken in Jamaica.

Best Places to Stay

Money Matters

Our accommodations price scale is designed to give you a ballpark figure for a typical stay during peak season. We've based these estimates on high season (December 15-April 15) for a standard room for two persons. These prices do not take into account options such as meal plans, dive packages, etc.

Port Antonio

Accommodations Price Scale

Prices are in US dollars.

Deluxe. . . . . $300+
Expensive . . . . $200-$300
Moderate . . . . $100-$200
Inexpensive. . . . . Under $100

Resorts

TRIDENT VILLAS AND HOTEL
Point Ann
☎ 876-993-2602, fax 876-993-2590
Reservations: ☎ 800-428-4734
Deluxe

This longtime favorite of the well-heeled crowd is one of Port Antonio's top resorts. The atmosphere here is super-quiet (when we had lunch here we were the only diners, except for a few elegant peacocks that strolled through the open-air restaurant). Look around for familiar celebrity faces; this is the kind of resort that has long drawn stars to Jamaica.

Adjacent to Trident is the Castle, a building of true castle proportions. Weekly guest parties are held here, as well as special events.

Guest rooms are elegant and private; dining here is white-gloved and equally cultivated. There is a small beach area, but most of the property is bordered by rugged rocks which are pounded by the sea night and day, truly a stunning sight. It is well worth coming out just for a look around the property and a meal.

JAMAICA PALACE
Drapers
☎ 876-993-7720
Reservations: ☎ 800-423-4095

Jamaica Palace is probably the most unusual property in Port Antonio, built like a 17th-century Italian palace. The black and white floor tiles that surround the exterior echo the black lacquered furniture inside.

Jamaica Palace is known for its unusual pool, which is built in the shape of the island itself.

Intimate Inns

BLUE LAGOON VILLAS
Fairy Hill
☎ 876-993-8491, fax 876-993-8492
Reservations: ☎ 800-822-3274
www.portantonio.com-blmain.htm
Deluxe

This is one of the most photographed accommodations in eastern Jamaica. One- , two- , three- , and four-bedroom villas are perched right on the water's edge, offering exquisite luxury and privacy. Each includes indoor and outdoor dining, a full kitchen, sun decks, daily housekeeping, meals served by the resident maid-chef and butler, and more. The villas are within swimming distance of the Blue Lagoon and Pelou Island, once owned by Princess Nina Aga Khan.

Blue Lagoon is for those in search of the ultimate getaway.

Port Antonio

DRAGON BAY
Point Ann
☎ 876-993-8751, fax 876-993-3284
Reservations: ☎ 800-633-3284
Expensive

These 30 villas are perched on a private lagoon. Choose from one, two or three bedrooms, each with beautiful surrounding gardens and all the comforts of home.

GOBLIN HILL VILLAS AT SAN SAN
Drapers
☎ 876-925-8108, fax 876-925-6248
Reservations: ☎ 800-472-1148
Expensive

There are two tennis courts at Goblin Hill lighted for night play.

Goblin Hill overlooks San San Bay, Port Antonio's beautiful harbor, and offers its guests peace and quiet. The 28 villas include the services of a housekeeper-cook who will serve up any of your favorite dishes. The villas are a short walk away from the water.

HOTEL MOCKING BIRD HILL
Point Ann
☎ 876-993-7267, fax 876-993-7133
Moderate to Expensive

This 10-room hotel is often cited for its ecofriendly policies – solar energy, locally produced furniture, natural landscaping. Even the restaurant, the excellent Mille Fleurs, features local produce. This property is very popular with ecotourists and offers many tours that explore the natural attractions of the Port Antonio area.

Best Places to Eat

For dining, we've set up a price scale based on a three-course dinner, including appetizer or soup, an entrée, dessert and coffee. Cocktails and wine are extra.

Dining Price Scale

Prices are per person in US dollars.

Expensive. . . . . $40+ per person
Moderate . . . . $25-$40
Inexpensive. . . . . Under $25

Recommended Restaurants

BLUE LAGOON
Fairy Hill
☎ 876-993-8491
Expensive

This casual eatery, located right beside the lagoon itself, serves authentic Jamaican dishes. Choose from jerk chicken or jerk sausage, vegetarian pizza, fresh lobster and more. Open daily for lunch and dinner. Live entertainment keeps Blue Lagoon hopping on weekends.

Port Antonio

DEVON HOUSE'S I SCREAM
West Street
Inexpensive

The ever-popular Kingston ice cream parlor also has a location in tiny Port Antonio (a clue to the popularity of this seaside getaway with Kingstonians). Cool off with a scoop of one of the many tropical flavors.

MILLE FLEURS
Hotel Mocking Bird Hill
☎ 876-993-7267 or 993-7134
Expensive

Mille Fleurs has been recommended by Gourmet magazine.

This restaurant overlooking Port Antonio and the Caribbean Sea is a romantic favorite. Sit on the terrace surrounded by tropical vegetation and enjoy the sunset (manager Shireen Aga recommends that guests arrive by 6 pm to enjoy cocktails and a sunset view). The restaurant offers an à la carte menu that changes daily. Lunch is served from noon to 2 pm; dinner is served starting at 7 pm, with the last order taken at 9:30.

Some of the interesting entrées served here include: chicken in June plum sauce; grilled fish with spicy mango-shrimp sauce; and spiced fish with tamarind and coconut sauce.

TRIDENT VILLAS AND HOTEL
Point Ann
☎ 876-993-2602
Expensive

Jackets are required for men at Trident.

This elegant eatery is the fanciest in Port Antonio. Dine by candlelight on either continental or Jamaican fare. Open daily for dinner.

Sunup to Sundown

Port Antonio is where people come to get away from everything, so don't expect a full array of nightlife and duty-free shopping here. You will find plenty of outdoor activity, however.

Beaches

Located at Boston Bay about 11 miles east of Port Antonio, **Boston Beach** is one of the area's most popular. Along with jerk stands, you'll see people surfing on some days.

Navy Beach, out on Navy Island, is accessible by ferry, which costs about US$3 per person.

San San Beach is five miles east of Port Antonio. The actual beach is small, but water is beautiful.

Blue Lagoon is not really a beach, but with water this pretty, who cares? Blue Lagoon is a must while you're in the Port Antonio area. Bring your towel and stay for the day.

Frenchman's Cove in Port Antonio is one of the best beaches on the island. This stretch of sand is very popular with locals. Free.

Port Antonio

Biking

Some of the island's most challenging bike rides are found in the Blue Mountains and on the roads south of Port Antonio. If you're

up to the challenge, you can rent a bike from **D & L Rentals**, ☎ 876-993-3282, or **Rainbow Rentals**, ☎ 876-993-2248.

Guided bicycle tours of the Blue Mountains are also available. Check with **Blue Mountain Bicycle Tours Ltd.** in Ocho Rios (☎ 876-974-7075 or 974-7492, fax 876-974-0635) for information on their Blue Mountain rides. These downhill tours have been featured in many magazines and include brunch, lunch, refreshments and all bike equipment. The tours cover 18 miles, all downhill, through the Blue Mountains and the tropical rain forest.

Fishing

Port Antonio is a favorite of deep-sea anglers. Home of the Blue Marlin Tournament, the quiet community is one of the top destinations for those in search of tuna, kingfish, wahoo and dolphin. Check with your hotel for local operators or call the *Bonita II*, ☎ 876-993-3086.

Sights & Attractions

BLUE LAGOON
One mile east of San San Beach
Open daily
☎ 876-993-8491
Admission

This beautiful sight is one that has to be seen to be believed. The cool, spring-fed waters cry out to swimmers. Floating docks encourage you to sun a little or you can lie out on the small beach. After a swim, try some Jamaican dishes in the casual lagoon-side restaurant.

BOSTON BEACH
11 miles east of Port Antonio
Open daily
Free

Boston Beach is known as the home of jerk and is a great place to head for a casual lunch. After a spicy meal, take a dip in the sea.

> ### ⚠ WARNING
>
> Be wary of waves at Boston Beach, which are often high enough for surfing.

FIREFLY
Port Marin
Hours: 8:30 am - 5:30 pm
☎ 800-OUTPOST

The land on which Firefly sits was originally sold to Noel Coward by Chris Blackwell's mother. After the playwright's death, the property was given to the Jamaican government; today Chris Blackwell leases the historic site and manages tours.

NAVY ISLAND
☎ 876-993-2667
Open daily
Admission

Spend a day on the island once owned by actor Errol Flynn. It's just a seven-minute boat ride from the mainland to this hideaway, which is home to several small cottages, a bar and a watersports operator. The ferry operates around the clock from West Street Harbor.

NONSUCH CAVES AND ATHENRY GARDEN
☎ 876-993-3740
Hours: 10 am - 4:30 pm daily
Admission

The three-acre Athenry Gardens are home to the Nonsuch Caves, filled with stalactites and stalagmites. The caves can be seen on a guided walk along well-lit passageways. The gardens are especially nice, with many local species accompanied by mountain views.

RIO GRANDE RAFTING
☎ 876-993-5778
Hours: 8:30 am - 4:30 pm daily, except Christmas and Good Friday

This river ride was the first in Jamaica and still the most famous. Wear your swimsuit if you'd like to take a dip in the river.

If you'd like to do a little shopping, just ask your captain to pull over at one of the stands. As you head down the river, be prepared for entrepreneurs to offer you everything from Red Stripe ("one for you and one for your captain?"), overpriced Pepsis, carved bamboo cups, flowers, birdfeeders made of carved coconut husks, whistles made of bamboo canes and more.

The ride is especially recommended in late afternoon (rafts stop about 3 pm) when you'll enjoy the sounds of frogs and crickets, sometimes deafening, from the river banks. In the late afternoon the banks come alive with the activity of the rural residents who use this waterway for everything from clothes washing to bathing to fishing. On a recent trip we watched two young boys spearfishing along one stretch, a woman doing the weekend washing on rocks around another bend, and a young boy catching fish by hand under the muddy banks.

The complete ride takes about 2½ hours (less if the river is up).

◎ TIP

Raftsmen expect a tip at the completion of the journey; US $5-$10 is appropriate.

Shop Till You Drop

Port Antonio has one notable shopping area: the **Village of St. George Shopping Centre**. Located on West Street, the building was designed using architecture from around the world to represent the many cultures that built Jamaica. This center is a good place for souvenirs, unique gifts and some food items.

Port Antonio

 # Port Antonio A-Z

Emergency Phone Numbers

Ambulance 110
Police. 119
Fire 110

Hospital

Port Antonio General Hospital
Naylor's Hill, Port Antonio
☎ 876-993-2646

Optometrists

Broadbent Jamaica Lmt.
City Centre Plaza
☎ 876-993-3618

Negril

Introduction

Since its early days as a haven for hippies in the 1970s, Negril has long harbored an image as a "wild" vacation destination. Nudity is common on the beaches of **Bloody Bay**, home to Hedonism II, a resort where the level of fun matches its tantalizing name. Reggae clubs bring some of the island's best music to the cliffs that overlook spectacular sunsets. And, while not as popular as it was during the 70s, more than one establishment still sells hallucinogenic teas and vendors still hawk ganja.

The real wildness in Negril lies just outside the city limits. Here, in an area known as the **Great Morass**, you can see a side of Jamaica that most visitors never glimpse. Here, crocodiles, not vacationers, lie in the steamy afternoon sunshine. Peddlers sell, not marijuana, but shrimp caught using techniques over 400 years old. And spectacular birds, not parasailers, fill the air with dashes of color and a cacophony of exotic sounds.

Today, Negril has gained respectability and is home to all types of resorts that attract everyone from swingers to families. Law mandates that no building here can be taller than a palm tree so the look is low rise, following the coast from Bloody Bay (named for the days when the whalers cleaned their catch here) to the cliffs at its southern end, where the Negril Lighthouse still signals the rocks to ships.

Negril is best known for its seven miles of beach, home to the largest share of accommodations and plenty of small restaurants. Travelers staying along this stretch can walk the beach from property to property.

FIVE-DAY NEGRIL ITINERARY	
Day One	Head to Negril for fun along the seven-mile beach. Catch a live reggae show at one of the beach clubs in the evening.
Day Two	Enjoy some watersports on the beach in the morning. In the afternoon, head into town for some shopping at the crafts market.
Day Three	Take a day trip to Black River and cruise to see the crocodiles.
Day Four	Spend the morning on the beach. In the afternoon, take a river raft trip at Lethe. Watch sunset from Negril's cliffs.
Day Five	Return to the cliffs and climb the lighthouse for the best view of Negril. Spend the rest of the day on the beach.

★ **DID YOU KNOW?**

Booby Cay on the north end of Negril doubled as the South Sea for Disney's *Twenty Thousand Leagues Under the Sea* movie.

Negril is a one- to two-hour drive from Montego Bay. Presently, the road is being rebuilt to straighten out many of the curves and speed up the drive. It will become a better route, but be aware that the construction can cause delays right now.

Many travelers on a tight schedule opt to take an intraisland flight from Montego Bay. It's about a 17-minute flight to the Negril airport, located across the street from Couples Ocho Rios, Grand Lido Negril and Hedonism II. From the airport, taxis are available to take you to any resort. For information on intraisland flights from either Montego Bay or Kingston, see the *Introduction*.

Getting Around

Car & Jeep Rentals

Remember, you'll drive on the left side of the road. You'll find several rental agencies in Negril, including:

Look RIGHT before crossing the street!

NEGRIL CAR RENTAL AGENCIES	
Dollar Rent-A-Car	☎ 876-957-4110
Paradise Jeep and Car Rental	☎ 876-957-4213
Safari Auto Rental	☎ 876-957-3306

Negril

Taxis

Taxis are the most popular method of transportation for travelers. They can be caught at any hotel, the airports, and most shopping areas. Travelers should be careful to use only licensed taxis; these have a red license plate that indicates the taxi is a Public Passenger Vehicle (PPV). If you need to call a taxi, contact the official carrier: Jamaica Union of Travelers Association or **JUTA** (☎ 876-957-9197 in Negril).

Few of Ja-maica's taxis are metered.

Taxi rates vary, but are figured by car, not by passenger. Fares average about US$5-7 for 10 miles.

⊚ TIP

If you accept a driver's offer of his services as a tour guide, be sure to agree on a price before the vehicle is put into gear.

Bus Service

This popular mode of transport for locals can be crowded and slow. The buses are generally not air-conditioned. Buses will stop anywhere along the route to pick up passengers. To catch one, stand by the side of the road with your arm outstretched; pat down with your hand when you see an oncoming bus. Bus fare is very inexpensive – about US$1 for 30-40 miles.

Orientation

Negril is Jamaica's most laid-back resort destination and the layout of the community shows it. The town sprawls along its chief attraction: a seven-mile stretch of beach that's one of the best in the Caribbean. On the north edge, enterting from Montego Bay, the resorts begin at **Bloody Bay**, a small bay that's home to several of the top resorts, including Grand Lido Negril, Hedonism II and Sandals Negril. This stretch of beach is across the street from the Negril airport, behind which lies a giant swamp called the **Great Morass**.

As you continue south, Bloody Bay gives way to **Long Bay**, home of the seven-mile-long Negril Beach. Along this stretch lie both big name resorts such as Beaches Negril and Poinciana Beach Resort as well as small inns under 50 rooms (and many much smaller). Travelers enjoy walking along the beach for

Negril

miles and will find many beach bars and restaurants on the sand. The resorts all lie on **Norman Manley Boulevard**, the main thoroughfare through the area, dividing the beach from the Great Morass.

Heading south, the beach is eventually broken by the intersection of the **South Negril River**, which marks the entrance to the town of Negril. Just north of the river lies the **Negril Crafts Market**, a ramshackle collection of buildings filled with woodcarvings, paintings, handmade jewelry, and really representing the spirit of Negril.

Often overlooked by travelers in recent years, the market is a fun place to stop in for a half-hour or so.

South of the market lies the roundabout and Norman Manley Boulevard becomes **West End Road**. To the east, Sheffield Road turns toward Savanna-La-Mar (known locally as Sav-La-Mar). West End Road continues south and traces the shoreline, which becomes less sandy and more rocky.

Look for local fishing boats in this area.

Eventually the rocky shoreline gives way to steep cliffs. Here lie some of Negril's budget getaways that are favored by young travelers as well as many longtime Negril fans. Many of the small properties are built right out on the cliffs and one even utilizes the sea caves as guest rooms. Along this stretch is the **Negril Lighthouse**, which offers the best view of the region (if you don't mind the climb).

Best Places to Stay

Room prices vary greatly with type of accommodation, location, and time of year. High season (mid-December through mid-April) brings
prices about 40% higher than in summer months.

Money Matters

Our price scale is designed to give you a ballpark
figure for a typical stay during peak season in a
standard room for two persons. These prices do
not take into account options such as meal plans
or dive packages.

Accommodations Price Scale

Prices are in US dollars.

Deluxe. . . . . $300+
Expensive . . . . $200-$300
Moderate . . . . $100-$200
Inexpensive. . . . . Under $100

*Be sure to con-
serve water, a
precious com-
modity on the
island.*

All our hotel selections take major credit cards,
are air-conditioned and have private baths, except in the case of the few guest houses where
noted.

Negril

Resorts

BEACHES NEGRIL
West End Road
☎ 876-957-9270, fax 876-957-9269
Reservations: ☎ 800-BEACHES
Expensive (All-inclusive)

Located on Long Bay, this is one of the newest members of the Sandals family. Unlike the Sandals resorts, however, Beaches is for everyone: families, singles and couples. The 225-room property includes five specialty restaurants and plenty of options for fun ranging from scuba diving to video games at the Sega Center.

COUPLES NEGRIL
Norman Manley Boulevard
Reservations: ☎ 800-268-7537
www.couples.com
Expensive (All-inclusive)

This is the newest resort in Negril, a couples-only property that exudes a relaxed Caribbean atmosphere. As with Couples Ocho Rios, everything is included, from top shelf liquors to watersports to transfers, as well as some off-property tours.

⊚ TIP

Be sure to ask about the package deal combining a stay at Couples Ocho Rios with Couples Negril.

GRAND LIDO NEGRIL
Norman Manley Boulevard
☎ 876-957-5011, fax 876-957-5517
Reservations: ☎ 800-467-8737
www.superclubs.com
Expensive to Deluxe (All-inclusive)

Part of the SuperClubs chain, this elegant resort is for overachievers who want to relax and kick back on the beach, but still enjoy 24-hour room service, top shelf liquors and all the amenities of a fine resort. Grand Lido is especially proud of its *MY Zein*, a 147-foot yacht that takes guests on sunset cruises.

★ **DID YOU KNOW?**

The yacht was originally a wedding gift from Aristotle Onassis to Prince Rainier and Princess Grace.

Daily lessons are offered in snorkeling, scuba diving, tennis and water skiing. For something less strenuous, there's the white sand beach for lazy (and, along one stretch, nude) sunbathing or satellite TV back in the room. Recently, the property has added a new spa and completed construction on 10 new suites, including a presidential suite with private outdoor Jacuzzi. The resort presently offers tennis, a fitness center, windsurfing, transfers to and from Negril Hills Country Club, watersports and a meeting facility for up to 200 attendees.

Guests at Grand Lido can indulge with a complimentary manicure or pedicure.

Negril

HEDONISM II
Norman Manley Bulevard
☎ 876-957-5200, fax 876-957-5289
Reservations: ☎ 800-859-7873
www.superclubs.com
Expensive (All-inclusive)

Hedonism II is a unique resort. It's definitely not for everyone, but for those who like its party-around-the-clock atmosphere, there's no place quite like it.

Hedonism II brings travelers from around the world who are looking for that teen-fun feeling in an adults-only version. Guests are tempted with Bacchanalian feasts, bars open until 5 am, a disco that closes when the last reveler calls it quits and clothing-optional beaches. Every night is a party, and the biggest blowout occurs on Thursday.

Toga Delight!

Every Thursday afternoon, maids deliver white sheets to guest rooms, but not for the beds. They're for the guests to wear to dinner that night. "No sheet, no eat" is the motto of the toga party, where some guests fashion traditional modest Roman wraps, but variations abound. You'll see women lining up at the buffet wearing topless micro-togas or men leaning against the bar sporting getups rarely seen outside a sumo wrestling ring. Hedonism's credo is that "a vacation should be whatever you want it to be," and for some that means a break from the cares and even the clothes of the everyday world.

Although some form of dress is required in the dining rooms, many guests wear only suntan oil and shades on the beach. The wide, white sand beach has room for everyone. Half of the sand is designated as "formal," with swimsuit required. The rest of the beach is reserved for those seeking the total tan. The nude beach has its own hot tub, bar and grill, cabanas and even volleyball and shuffleboard courts. The beach is the focal point of the resort, and it's part of seven miles of white sand for which Negril is best known.

Located on 22 acres, Hedonism II offers plenty of natural beauty. A few barefoot steps from the sea, coconut palms, flowering hibiscus and banana trees create a mood of seclusion and privacy.

After dinner, there's a nightly show organized by the resort's entertainment crew. You'll see guests and staff strut their stuff during talent night (which might include an amateur strip-tease), fly through the air during the circus show, or bend over backwards for the limbo contest. It's in these after-dark hours when the hedonists really get busy. Following the night's party, guests head to a disco that flashes with a $500,000 lighting system or to the nude hot tub for late night revelry. Eventually even the party-till-you-drop crowd heads back to their rooms, which at Hedonism are comfortable but not luxurious.

Rooms at Hedonism II have mirrored ceilings above every bed.

SANDALS NEGRIL
Norman Manley Boulevard
☎ 800-726-3257 or 876-957-5216, fax 876-957-5338
www.sandals.com
Expensive (All-inclusive)

Negril

Part of the popular Sandals couples-only chain that originated in Jamaica, this resort is popular with young, sports-oriented couples. Watersports are a big offering and the resort even includes one pool just for scuba lessons. Tennis, racquetball, squash and other activities are included for land-lubbers.

Like other resorts in the Sandals chain, Sandals Negril offers guests the "Stay at One, Dine at Six" policy. Guests can dine at other Sandals resorts if they venture to Montego Bay or Ocho Rios.

SWEPT AWAY
Norman Manley Boulevard
☎ 800-545-7937 or 876-957-4061, fax 876-957-4060
Expensive (All-inclusive)

Swept Away has a three-night minimum stay and has one of the best sports and fitness resorts in Jamaica.

Swept Away Negril is now part of the Issa Resort Collection and has converted from a couples-only to an adults-only policy. The 134-suite property offers a 10-acre sports complex with 10 lit tennis courts (two with stadium seating), racquetball, squash, basketball, a gym and more. A full-service spa, watersports, scuba diving, unlimited golf at the Negril Hills Golf Club are all part of the package. The resort includes a conference center for up to 120 attendees.

Swept Away markets itself to fitness and health-conscious couples. Dining here includes many healthy choices, including Feathers (see below).

Hotels

DEVINE DESTINY
Summerset Road
☎ 876-957-9184, fax 876-957-3846
Inexpensive to Moderate

This hotel is especially popular with Europeans as well as vacationing Jamaicans. Although it sits away from the beach, a free shuttle service is available. Built around a beautiful pool area, the rooms each include refrigerators and have air-conditioning or ceiling fans (make your requests if this is important to you).

NEGRIL CABINS RESORT
Norman Manley Boulevard
☎ 876-957-5350, fax 876-957-5381
Moderate to Expensive

Negril is bordered to the east by the Great Morass. This swampland is rich with peat, a substance that was considered as a possible energy source in the 1970s when scientists studied the feasibility of mining this resource. Environmental concerns about the possibility of damaging Negril's famous Seven Mile Beach put a stop to the mining plans.

Negril Cabins offers tours to the Royal Palms Reserve, located directly behind the property.

During the study of the Morass, these researchers lived in cabins in Negril. Today, Negril Cabins utilizes those original structures plus several new buildings and operates as a resort for those want to combine the luxuries of a hotel with the natural experience of camping. Visitors enjoy Swiss Family Robinson-style accommodations in cabins perched on stilts. Lush grounds are filled with in-

Negril

digenous Jamaican flora and fauna and dotted with colorful hummingbirds.

Children under 12 stay free with an adult at the cabins.

Units here include 24 standard rooms with telephone, ceiling fan, private shower and private balcony. More than 60 air-conditioned superior rooms include satellite TV.

The resort includes the Coconut Palm Restaurant, the Alfresco Restaurant for buffet dinners Monday through Friday nights, a bar and grill at poolside and a beach snack bar.

NEGRIL GARDENS
Norman Manley Boulevard
☎ 876-957-4408, fax 876-957-4374
Moderate to Expensive (All-inclusive optional)

This resort has an all-inclusive plan, but can also be booked as an EP (meals-only) stay, dinner only or breakfast and dinner. With 66 rooms, this pink two-story resort is situated on both sides of Norman Manley Boulevard.

Intimate Inns

THE CAVES
West End Road, Negril
☎ 800-OUTPOST
www.islandlife.com
Deluxe

At this tranquil property, guests fall asleep to the sound of waves echoing through the namesake for this inn, sea caves formed from ancient volcanic rock and the pounding surf.

In the day, vacationers leave one of five hand-crafted cottages and snorkel among these grottos and caves or sun on the decks among the cliffs. A special treat is a massage in the sea cave, during which you can listen to the undulating waves.

Like Straw-berry Hill, this Island Outpost property is owned by record producer Chris Blackwell.

The Caves offers Aveda services from massage to an invigorating sea salt glow using salts from the Dead Sea. Breakfast and lunch are served beneath a thatched palapa and dinner is available by arrangement.

CHARELA INN
Norman Manley Boulevard
☎ 876-957-4277, fax 876-957-4414
Moderate

This 49-room hotel sits right on the seven-mile-long beach in Negril. Its recently refurbished rooms are within steps of the sand; each has a private patio or balcony. The hotel is home to LaVendome Restaurant.

COCO LA PALM SEASIDE RESORT
Norman Manley Boulevard
☎ 876-957-4227, fax 876-957-3460
Reservations: ☎ 800-896-0987
www.cocolapalm.com
Moderate

Coco La Palm has a great location on Negril's main beach.

Coco La Palm is a quiet property with lush grounds and a beautiful stretch of beach. Our room, like most of those at the newly constructed resort, was large, and included a mini-refrigerator and a small patio. Home of the Seaside Bar and Grill.

Negril

ROCKHOUSE
West End Road
☎ 876-957-4373, fax 876-957-4373
Moderate to Expensive

Rockhouse is great for adults, but we don't recommended it for families with young children because of the cliffs.

Another small inn along Negril's cliffs is Rockhouse. Just steps from busy West End Road, once through the gates at Rockhouse you'll feel that you are tucked away from the world. The restaurant and bar are perched high on Negril's bluffs and look directly out to sea and an unbeatable sunset. Rooms here are constructed from wood, thatch and stone, like something out of *Gilligan's Island*. The natural theme of this resort is carried out in the open-air showers. This inn just added new studio rooms and a spectacular clifftop pool.

ROOT'S BAMBOO
Norman Manley Boulevard
☎ 876-957-4479
Inexpensive

Take a self-contained room or toss your own tent at this casual spot, which is also home to Bamboo Restaurant.

SEA SPLASH RESORT
Norman Manley Boulevard
☎ 876-957-4041
Inexpensive

After a meal at Tan-ya's, the on-site restaurant, take a few minutes to look around Sea Splash Resort. This popular family destination offers 15 suites, each just steps from the beach.

Best Places to Eat

Money Matters

Visa, Mastercard, American Express, Diners Club and Access are commonly accepted; Discover is accepted at some establishments. Some restaurants add a 15% gratuity to the bill, so make sure you don't inadvertently tip twice.

For dining, we've set up a price scale based on a three-course dinner, including appetizer or soup, an entrée, dessert and coffee. Cocktails and wine are extra.

Dining Price Scale

Prices are per person in US dollars.

Expensive. . . . . $40+ per person
Moderate . . . . $25-$40
Inexpensive. . . . . Under $25

Recommended Restaurants

BAMBOO RESTAURANT
Root's Bamboo
Norman Manley Boulevard
☎ 876-957-4479
Inexpensive

Jamaican and international dishes are served at this casual eatery. If you're not hungry, just stop

Negril

by the Root's Bamboo Beach Bar for fun on the sand.

CASAVA TERRACE
Couples Negril
Norman Manley Boulevard
All-inclusive

The menu at Casava Terrace changes nightly.

Night passes are available for non-guests at Couples Negril, the latest addition to this resort community's all-inclusive offerings. The restaurant offers a fine selection of local cuisine. Choose from local favorites such as brown stew chicken, braised oxtail with broad beans, West Indian vegetarian roti, grilled lobster medallions with lime garlic butter, Creole Bloody Bay stew with okra, baked squirrel fish in banana leaves and, of course, rice and peas.

COCONUT PALM RESTAURANT
Negril Cabins Resort
Norman Manley Boulevard
☎ 876-957-5350
Moderate to Expensive

We have fond memories of this open-air eatery that bring back the spicy tastes of Jamaica and the joy of dining beneath the stars. Jamaican dishes grace this menu, all served by a talented chef.

COSMO'S SEAFOOD RESTAURANT AND BAR
Norman Manley Boulevard
☎ 876-957-4330
Moderate to Expensive

Cosmo's is a long-time favorite with Negril travelers looking for good seafood. Super casual, the restaurant is right on the beach and folks wander in and out on their way to the sand and sea.

Cosmo's specialties include conch, lobster and fresh daily catches.

DA BUSS
Norman Manley Boulevard
☎ 876-957-4405
Inexpensive

This restaurant is easy to find: just look for the bus. The colorful double decker transport once starred in a Bond flick; now it takes a lead role in casual Negril dining with jerk and other local favorites.

FEATHERS CONTINENTAL RESTAURANT
Swept Away
Norman Manley Boulevard
☎ 876-957-4061
All-inclusive

Swept Away opens its restaurant to non-guests.

Fine dining is the order of the day at Feathers, the gourmet restaurant of Swept Away. Menu offerings start with pan-seared sweetbreads in a vermouth reduction, Courvoisier escargot in crisped phyllo and Cornish game hen galantine on a berry and lemon grass relish. Entrées range from baked Black River crayfish to ackee-enhanced vegetable bolognaise to roasted loin of pork with a grain mustard accompanied by mango chutney.

Reservations are required to dine at Feathers, usually 24 hrs in advance.

KIMONOS
Sandals Negril
Norman Manley Boulevard
☎ 876-957-5216
All-inclusive

This couples-only restaurant features Teppanyaki-style dining; chefs prepare meals right at the table. Start with Caribbean-style sushi, Cantonese

Negril

spring rolls, or crab and sweet corn soup. Don't worry about making choices for the entrée; the chef prepares a feast of sesame chicken breast, strip steak sukiyaki, pepper, sherry tiger shrimp, pork tenderloin Caribe, ginger teppan scallops, and glazed marlin teriyaki served with sushi rice and stir-fried vegetables.

KUYABA ON THE BEACH
Norman Manley Boulevard
☎ 876-957-4318
Inexpensive to Moderate

Kuyaba offers free pick-up from area hotels.

Dine on international dishes with a Jamaican flair. The mood here is as casual as can be; feel free to go from the restaurant right out to the beach.

LAVENDOME RESTAURANT
Charela Inn
Norman Manley Boulevard
☎ 876-957-4277
Expensive

Dine inside or outdoor just steps off the sand at this fun restaurant that features Jamaican dishes with a French twist.

MARGUERITAVILLE
Norman Manley Boulevard
☎ 876-957-4467
Moderate to Expensive

Margueritaville is a popular spring break spot.

Like its sister restaurant in Montego Bay, this new establishment is a place for rowdy fun. The super casual restaurant is better known for its party atmosphere than its food. Look for a Frisbee golf course, volleyball, basketball and a beach club. Oh, yeah, there's food, too: burgers, sandwiches, fish, chicken and lobster, not to mention over 50 types of margaritas.

ORCHID TERRACE RESTAURANT
Negril Gardens
Norman Manley Boulevard
☎ 876-957-4408
Moderate

This casual restaurant offers dining with a different theme every night. On Wednesday night, enjoy a beach barbecue; Sunday is Jamaican night, featuring the Ashanti Dancers in a spectacular show.

Call ahead to find out the theme of the night at Orchids.

OTAHEITE
Couples Negril
Norman Manley Boulevard
☎ 876-957-5370
All-inclusive

Otaheite is the fine dining restaurant at Couples Negril, with a gourmet twist on local cuisine. Chefs really outdo themselves with the entrées, which marry Jamaican ingredients and gourmet talents. Some of the mouth-watering dishes are: pan-seared Atlantic salmon with jerk coating; grilled lamb shoulder chops; wild rabbit; and Ethiopian doro wot. Doro wot is the national dish of Abyssinia, a skinless chicken stew with a blend of Ethiopian spices. Like the resort itself, this is a couples-only restaurant.

Negril

PIACERE
Grand Lido Negril
Norman Manley Boulevard
☎ 876-957-5011
All-inclusive

*Piacere requires
that men wear
jackets.*

*We loved our
dinner here.
Piacere really
stands out in
our memories.*

This elegant eatery is one of the best all-inclusive
restaurants on the island, and (unlike the other
fine dining restaurants at SuperClubs resorts) is
available only to guests of Grand Lido Negril.
Start the meal with chausson of duck confit; sliv-
ers of home-smoked pork tenderloin; seafood
symphony pancake; or chilled mango nectar.
Entrées are equally intriguing: tournedos of
Black Angus beef tenderloin; grilled swordfish
grenadine; roasted Provimi veal chop; pan-fried
pavé of deep sea halibut; and roast crown of lamb.

Finish off the evening with a taste of Blue Mountain coffee and a decadent dessert.

PICKLED PARROT RESTAURANT
West End Road
☎ 876-957-4864
Moderate

The Pickled Parrot is the kind of place you come to
get, well, pickled. Known for its spring break atmosphere, you can't miss the restaurant if you're
out boating along the cliffs: just look for the
waterslide. A great place for a sunset dinner, to
enjoy American, Jamaican and Mexican dishes.

The Pickled Parrot is not a good place for families
with young children because of the steep cliffs
close by. We visited this restaurant with our teen-
ager recently, though, and the place was a big hit,
both for its waterslide and its rop swing off the
cliff.

RICK'S CAFE
West End Road
☎ 876-957-0380
Moderate

Known as Negril's top sunset bar, Rick's is also a popular restaurant. Filet mignon, kingfish, broiled lobster, jerk chicken, coco bread pizza and blackened chicken breast are served in the open-air dining room. It's not the best restaurant in Negril and definitely not the place to go for a quiet, romantic dinner (the daredevils jumping off the cliffs take care of that), but it is always a fun hangout and a terrific spot to watch the sunset.

Bring cash; Rick's does not accept credit cards.

Arrive at Rick's early if you'd like a table by the edge for the best view.

THE ROCKHOUSE RESTAURANT AND BAR
Rockhouse
West End Road
☎ 876-957-4373
Moderate

Breakfast, lunch and dinner are served at this open-air eatery. It's just steps from busy West End Road but, once through the gates at Rockhouse and seated beneath the restaurant's thatched roof, you are tucked away from the world.

We recommend that you make reservations for dinner at the Rockhouse.

The restaurant and bar are perched high on Negril's bluffs and look directly out to sea and an unbeatable sunset. Jamaican cuisine with European influences is the specialty here. This restaurant is an excellent choice for a romantic dinner with real Negril style.

Negril

SEASIDE BAR AND GRILL
Coco La Palm Seaside Resort
Norman Manley Boulevard
☎ 876-957-4227
Inexpensive to Moderate

This open-air restaurant is one of Negril's best. A diverse menu keeps things interesting, with Jamaican specialties transformed into culinary masterpieces.

Menu selections include coconut-crusted snapper on a bed of callaloo; rum and lime broiled chicken breast with honey-lime butter; and jerk festival fettucine.

SEVILLE
Beaches Negril
West End Road
☎ 876-957-9270
All-inclusive

Reservations are required and dressy attire is suggested for a night at Seville.

Non-guests can buy a night pass for Beaches Negril and select from one of several restaurants including this Jamaican eatery. Here, white-gloved attendants serve Jamaican dishes prepared with a gourmet flair. Menu selections include jerked salmon filet; grilled beef tenderloin; lamb loin Wellington; pimento wood smoked pork loin; and pan-seared veal medallion.

THE SUNDOWNER
Sandals Negril
Norman Manley Boulevard
☎ 876-957-5216
All-inclusive

White-gloved service makes a meal at this eatery a special experience. The couples-only restaurant serves Caribbean cuisine starting with appetizers such as Bahamian conch salad, ackee and saltfish or Grenadian ham patty. Entrée options include Jamaican steamfish; Trinidadian roti; jerked suckling pig; West Indian cassoulet; and St. Vincent "Pelau," chicken sautéed in brown sugar and cooked with tomato, peas and rice.

TEPPANYAKI
Beaches Negril
West End Road
☎ 876-957-9270
All-inclusive

We recently enjoyed a great dinner here. Diners are entertained by their chef, making this a combination show and dinner. Entrées are prepared at the table by a teppanyaki chef and include chicken breast yakitori infused with lemongrass, dry sherry, ginger, sesame oil and spring onions; pork filet "Loisin Jeung" brushed with Hoisin sauce and finished with toasted cashews; and beef teriyaki marinated in a light soy sauce and enhanced with honey, garlic and pickled ginger.

Both children and adults are made welcome at Teppanyaki.

Kids enjoy the "Junior Emperor's Platter" with vegetable spring rolls, and chicken nuggets and breaded shrimp served with apricot and honey dip.

Local Foods

THE HUNGRY LION
West End Road
☎ 876-957-4486
Inexpensive to Moderate

Negril

The Hungry Lion is a great place to try Ital dishes.

This relaxed place serves excellent vegetarian cuisine. Dishes such as a meatless shepherd's pie and pastas are flavorful.

SWEET SPICE
1 White Hall Road
☎ 876-957-4321
Inexpensive

We had a wonderful lunch at Sweet Spice, a real Jamaican eatery.

At Sweet Spice you'll be cooled by a small fan and the breeze that comes through the open doorway. Artwork on the blue tinted walls consists of framed towels with Jamaican axioms. But this restaurant is the real thing: a Jamaican diner with food to match. Conch steak, barbecued chicken and curried goat, shrimp and chicken are top offerings, served with rice. Cool off with a pawpaw daiquiri or a piña colada.

Dress cool for this warm eatery.

For a real taste of Jamaica home cooking, this restaurant is one of the best spots to visit in Negril.

TAN-YA'S
Sea Splash Resort
Norman Manley Boulevard
☎ 876-957-4041
Moderate

Save plenty of time for a meal at Tan-ya's... you'll need it. We enjoyed breakfast here, but were just about ready to start thinking about lunch when our plates came out. This is a small operation with an even a smaller kitchen, so don't expect fast food turnaround times. As Jamaicans often say, "soon come" and yes, it will soon come. Be patient. Enjoy the beautiful beach, take a walk if you like, and when it comes, your meal will be worth the wait.

We ordered ackee and bacon, a delightful twist on a traditional island favorite. It was one of the best breakfasts we've ever eaten. You can also have lunch or dinner in this super casual eatery where each table is tucked beneath its own palm-thatched roof.

Tan-ya's specials include deviled crab backs & smoked marlin.

Sunup to Sundown

Negril operates at a different pace than Jamaica's other resort areas. Sure, you'll find plenty of activity along its beaches – jetskiing, banana boat rides, parasailing, you name it – but the real action in Negril is relaxing.

Beaches

Negril is basically one long, seven-mile beach. This is as good as it gets for real beach devotees. The atmosphere here is still much like it has been for the past 30 years – relaxed, laid back and not too developed. Most of the seven miles of sand have been developed, but the facilities are small – quaint jerk stands, small outdoor eateries, a few guest houses sprinkled among the hotel properties. There's non-stop action along the beach and vendors can come up to the high water line but behind this line visitors can relax in peace and soak up the Negril atmosphere.

Nude & Topless Beaches

Nude beaches are found at **Hedonism II** and **Grand Lido Negril**; both have beach bars and grills.

Scuba Diving

Negril offers some of the best scuba diving in Jamaica. Call one of these operators for day and night dives:

DIVE OPERATORS	
Blue Whale Divers	☎ 876-957-4438
Dolphin Divers	☎ 876-957-4944
Hedonism II	☎ 876-957-5200
Negril Scuba Centre	☎ 876-957-4425
Sandals Resort	☎ 876-957-5216
Sundivers Negril	☎ 876-957-4331
West Point Watersports	☎ 876-957-5170

Fishing

Several operators offer excursions for deep-sea fishing excursions:

DEEP-SEA FISHING OPERATORS	
Best Boat Reef Tour	☎ 876-995-9709
Blue Whale Divers	☎ 876-957-4438
Sea Raider, Our Past Time	☎ 876-957-4224
Wild Thing, Mahogany Inn	☎ 876-957-4401 or 4402

Golf

NEGRIL HILLS
On the road to Savannah-La-Mar
☎ 876-957-4638

These rolling greens feature 18 holes, a club-house, bar, restaurant, pro shop and tennis.

Biking

Many of the larger properties have bicycles available for guest use; if yours doesn't, call one of these outfitters.

BICYCLE RENTALS	
Coco Bike Rental	☎ 876-957-4250
Dependable Bike Rental	☎ 876-957-4764
Elvie's Bike Rental	☎ 876-957-4331
Gas Bike Rental	☎ 876-957-4835
Holiday Bike Rental	☎ 876-957-4968
Jah B's Bike Rental	☎ 876-957-4235
Jolly's Bike Rental	☎ 876-957-3385
Kool Bike Rental Limited	☎ 876-957-9224
Nortigo Bike Rental	☎ 876-957-4711
Pedro Bike Rental	☎ 876-957-4757
Reid's Bike Rental	☎ 876-957-4369
Tykes Bike Rental	☎ 876-957-0388
Wright's Bike Rental	☎ 876-957-4908

Negril

⚠ WARNING

Traffic can be hectic on the busier stretches of Norman Manley Boulevard, so ride with care.

Sights & Attractions

ANANCY FUN PARK
Norman Manley Boulevard,
across from Beaches Inn
Hours: sunup to sundown
☎ 876-957-5100
Admission, per ride

Anancy Park welcomes families with an 18-hole miniature golf course, go-kart racetrack, carousel and power wheels for the youngest visitors. Families can also take a WaterSkeeter pontoon paddleboat in the small lake and youngsters can borrow a fishing pole to try their luck in the well-stocked pond.

NEGRIL LIGHTHOUSE
West End Road
Open daily
☎ 876-957-4875
Admission: tip

This 100-foot lighthouse is open for tours. Just stop by the caretaker's cottage next door and ask to see the it; the charge is just a tip.

Shop Till You Drop

Negril doesn't offer the extensive shopping of the cruise port cities of MoBay or Ocho Rios, but foodies will find some good stops. The **Hi-Lo Grocery Store**, on West End Road in the Hi-Lo Shopping Centre, is one of our favorite shopping stops on the island. Pop in to purchase spices, hot sauces and Blue Mountain coffee at prices far lower than you'll see in the hotel gift shops.

While you're at the shopping mall, walk from shop to shop for a good selection of souvenirs, liquor, local music, cigars and sportswear.

At press time, a new shopping area was opening called **Time Square** on Norman Manley Boulevard. This mall promises to bring the duty-free shopping that's formerly been found only in MoBay and along the coast from Ochi to Negril. Look for fine jewelry, watches, designer clothing, perfumes, leather goods and more.

⭐ **NOTE**

The mall at Time Square is officially open, although not all the shops are ready to do business.

Negril

Cigars

DIS AND DAT
Hi-Lo Shopping Centre
☎ 876-957-4916

This souvenir shop includes a walk-in humidor and offers numerous top brands: Cohiba, Monte Cristo, Hoya de Monterrey, Romeo y Julieta, Bolivar, Partagas, Macanudo, Royal Jamaican and more.

Local Crafts

Negril is home to the **Negril Crafts Market**, located just off Norman Manley Boulevard as you head south into town. The market isn't much to look at – a collection of rickety buildings – but the atmosphere is fun and there are some good crafts to be purchased if you persevere. We recently bought a very nice woodcarving here for US$12, along with some nice beaded jewelry starting at $3.

The market is much quieter than those in MoBay and Ocho Rios, so don't expect to hide in the masses – you will be spotted and asked (make that requested) to "come look at my things." Go with the flow, put a smile on your face, and enjoy the experience in good humor.

> ◎ **TIP**
>
> Bargaining is very much a part of the game; shoot for about half the asked price on most goods.

Gifts & Souvenirs

DIS AND DAT
Hi-Lo Shopping Centre
☎ 876-957-4916

Along with an extensive selection of cigars (see above), this souvenir shop offers coffee, t-shirts, local spices, rums, beach towels and other souvenir fare.

After Dark

Negril is known for its nightlife – not the glitzy, dress-up kind, but the funky, barefoot style that's the essence of Negril. You'll find that every night, one particular club is *the* place to be. Throughout the day, you'll often hear cars with loudspeakers driving up and down Norman Manley Boulevard announcing that night's show. As you walk through town, notice the neon-colored signs indicating upcoming acts.

We recommend asking your hotel concierge for the best spots. No concierge? No problem. Just about anyone in Negril can point you to the night's hot spot. We tested it out recently and everyone, from front desk people to the taxi drivers, knew the place to be on any given night.

Negril

Beach Shows

ALFRED'S OCEAN PALACE
Norman Manley Boulevard
☎ 876-957-4735

Wear your shorts and t-shirt for Alfred's, a genuine beach bar. The shows at Alfred's are held outside (actually, there's not really an inside). The crowd of both locals and tourists fills the beach.

Rent-A-Dread

In Negril, there's a particular occupation that's very apparent, especially during the evening shows. Call it male prostitution or the local nickname, Rent-A-Rasta or Rent-A-Dread. Young (and not so young) hustlers approach women of all ages (European women are favorite targets). They may be charming, they may offer to show you the "real" Jamaica, but the payoff's the same. "You take care of them, they take care of you," laughed one taxi driver when he explained the business arrangement.

KUYABA BEACH RESTAURANT AND BAR
Norman Manley Boulevard
☎ 876-957-4318

This eatery features all types of tropical music early in the evenings.

RISKY BUSINESS
Norman Manley Boulevard
☎ 876-957-3008

Like Alfred's, Risky Business is another happening reggae hotspot.

Disco

HEDONISM II
Norman Manley Boulevard
☎ 876-957-5200

There's no hotter place in Negril (or on the island, for that matter) than the disco at Hedonism II. You'll have to pay a hefty fee for a night pass, which includes all your drinks and food once you're on property. The disco features an incredible light and sound system and a rotating theme. The most popular night is Tuesday, when it's PJ night and anything goes – thong bikinis, bondage suits, you name it. The action doesn't start until after 11 and goes on until the last person staggers out of the disco.

Negril A-Z

Banks

Bank of Nova Scotia
Negril Square, Negril
☎ 876-957-3040

Negril

Currency Exchange

Currency exchange is offered at the larger resorts (at a rate usually slightly less favorable than the bank rate), at the banks, or at:

Time Trend Financial Co.
Norman Manley Boulevard
☎ 876-957-4974

Emergency Phone Numbers

Ambulance 110
Police. 119
Fire 110

Grocery Stores

Hi-Lo Food Store
West End Road
☎ 876-957-4546

Prices on imported items are quite a bit higher than you'd pay at home, thanks to duties.

This is more than a grocery store to us; it's also our favorite gift store. We buy all our Jamaican coffees, hot sauces, jerk sauces and rums here at prices far lower than in the gift stores. You'll also find all the usual grocery items.

Optical Services

Negril Vision Center
Kings Plaza (next to Hi-Lo)
☎ 876-957-3654

Pharmacies

Basic pharmaceutical items are sold at hotel gift shops and the grocery stores, but for special needs try:

Negril Pharmacy
Adrija Plaza
☎ 876-957-4076

Photo Labs

Can't wait to get your film developed when you get home? There are several labs in Negril, including:

Aqua Sun and Video
Plaza De Negril
☎ 876-957-9008

**Color Negril Photography,
Video and Lab Services**
Coral Seas Plaza
☎ 876-957-4594

Kingston

Introduction

The capital city of Kingston lies on the south shore. This metropolitan area of over 800,000 residents is visited primarily by business travelers. Within this sprawling metropolis, however, beats the true heart of Jamaica. Travelers interested in the culture and history that define this island nation should make time for a visit to Kingston, the largest English-speaking city south of Miami.

Kingston is not an easy city to love. It's big, brash and boisterous. Crime is a major problem, so severe that some taxi drivers won't even venture into the downtown region (more on that later). Life spills out from storefronts and homes onto the streets, filling the sidewalks and every inch of available space. Goats roam the downtown area, sidewalk vendors peddle all type of merchandise from carts and tables, pedestrians are everywhere.

Kingston dates back to 1692. The city is built along the harbor, stretching from the Blue Mountains in the east to the boundaries of Spanish Town to the west.

The Kingston Tourist

Kingston is not for everyone. It does not offer a relaxing, fun-in-the-sun vacation. Head to the North Coast resort communities for that type of getaway.

Instead, Kingston is for those travelers who want to really get to know Jamaica. If you've had a few dates with Jamaica and you're ready to visit her parents, then it's time to head to Kingston. Things aren't always pretty here, but it's a necessary part of the experience.

Kingston is recommended for travelers who:

- ◎ Are doing business in Jamaica.
- ◎ Are looking for the heart of the island's music business.
- ◎ Are seeking to learn more about Jamaican art and history.
- ◎ Want to combine the city experience with a look at the Blue Mountains.

Crime Alert

Kingston's crime statistics are legendary. Although not directed specifically at tourists, crime of all types does occur on a regular basis in the bustling city. Be on your guard.

Kingston itself is not one city but a conglomeration of communities and neighborhoods with invisible boundaries that are very clear to those who live here.

Many residents will not enter certain sections of the city. Just which sections should you avoid?

The worst regions are west and south of the city. Arriving from Spanish Town, the neighborhoods of **Six Miles** and **Riverton City** are some of the city's worst. South along the waterfront, Spanish Town Road skirts through the downtown, a high-crime district many Kingstonians will not visit, day or night.

Getting There

Most visitors fly into Kingston's Norman Manley International Airport, which is on a peninsula that faces the city. It's a half-hour drive into New Kingston (count on close to an hour if you're staying at the hotels up in the mountains like Strawberry Hill).

Getting Around

Car & Jeep Rentals

Before we give you the rental agencies in Kingston, this word of caution: think twice about renting a car here. Along with the usual Jamaica traffic problems (which range from goats in the road to king-size potholes), you'll be faced with a potential crime problem. At press time the city was experiencing severe problems with gangs. Murder rates have been on the rise, although tourists are not generally singled out.

Please reread the warning above regarding which sections of town to miss, and check with your hotel staff for current places to avoid.

With all that said, there are several car rental agencies in town.

KINGSTON CAR RENTAL AGENCIES	
Budget Car Rental	☎ 876-924-8762 or 924-8626 (Norman Manley Airport)
Econocar Rentals	☎ 876-927-676111 (Lady Musgrave Road)
Fiesta Car Rentals	☎ 876-926-013314 (Waterloo Road)
Island Car Rentals	☎ 876-926-5991 (17 Antigua Avenue)

Taxis

The best transportation option within Kingston is a taxi. You can catch one at any hotel, the airports, and in most shopping areas. Travelers should also be careful to only use licensed taxis; these have a red license plate that indicates the taxi as a Public Passenger Vehicle (PPV).

Taxi rates vary but are figured by car, not by passenger. Fares average about US$5-7 for 10 miles. Few of Jamaica's taxis are metered. If you accept a driver's offer of his services as a tour guide, be sure to agree on a price before the vehicle is put into gear.

Kingston Tours

Taxi tours are an excellent way to see the city. You can set your own itinerary and travel at your own pace. **Sun Island Tours and Limousine Service** (☎ 876-901-8826) offers guided tours.

Orientation

Along the waterfront is the commercial center of Kingston. Here, goods come and go from around the world. Farther east, the business section of downtown is home to many international corporations, consulate offices, banks, insurance companies and the world-class **Jamaica Convention Centre**. This is the home of the **International Seabed Authority**, the UN body that creates all laws for the world's seas. The modern center lies along the lovely waterfront on **Ocean Boulevard**, where parks overlook the harbor and you can enjoy an afternoon with the locals, dining on street food and absorbing the atmosphere.

Near the Jamaica Conference Centre, the waterfront becomes a pedestrian area, as people sit out and enjoy the sunshine, share conversation, and buy local foods from vendors.

Look out across the waters and you'll see a peninsula. This is where Norman Manley International Airport is located. Beyond the airport lies the fishing village of **Port Royal**, once one of the greatest cities in the Caribbean. Nicknamed "the wickedest city in Christendom," Port Royal was a hangout for the pirates of the Caribbean. All that rollicking fun came to a screeching halt on June 7, 1692, when a violent earthquake shook the region and pummeled Port Royal into the sea. Archaeologists have recovered artifacts from the scandalous community and today shoppers can buy reproductions of Port Royal pewter plates and cups from Things Jamaican (see *Shop Till You Drop*).

Plans are underway for big development in Port Royal, and will once again focus attention on the history of this area. They call for protection of the offshore cays, development of an historic interpretive master plan, construction of a cruise ship pier and arrival center, and the restoration of many historic buildings such as Fort Charles, the Old Naval Hospital, Victoria and Albert Battery, and more. For today, however, Port Royal is a quiet stop, just a small fishing village.

> ⊚ **TIP**
>
> If you're in Port Royal for the day, eat lunch at **Gloria's** fish shack, where you can sit on picnic tables under awning and enjoy fish: escovitch, fried or steamed.

Most Kingston travelers spend their time in **New Kingston**, north of the downtown area. Bounded

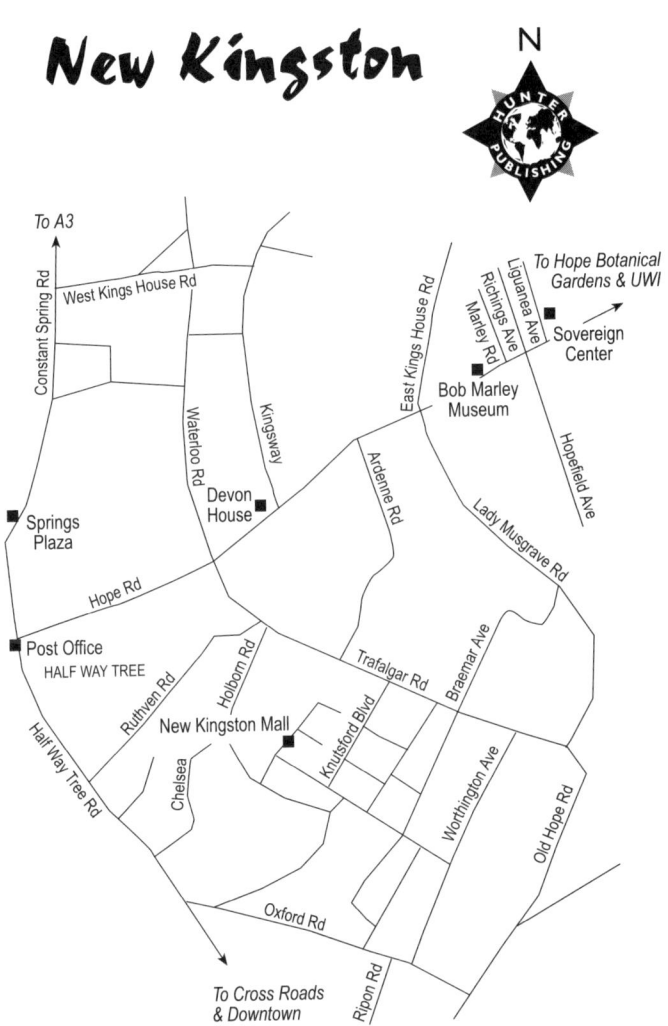

New Kingston

N

To A3

Constant Spring Rd

West Kings House Rd

East Kings House Rd

To Hope Botanical
Gardens & UWI

Liguanea Ave

Richings Ave

Marley Rd

Sovereign
Center

Waterloo Rd

Kingsway

Bob Marley
Museum

Ardenne Rd

Devon
House

Hopefield Ave

Springs
Plaza

Lady Musgrave Rd

Hope Rd

Post Office
HALF WAY TREE

Ruthven Rd

Holborn Rd

Trafalgar Rd

Braemar Ave

New Kingston Mall

Half Way Tree Rd

Chelsea

Knutsford Blvd

Worthington Ave

Old Hope Rd

Oxford Rd

To Cross Roads
& Downtown

Ripon Rd

NOT TO SCALE

by Old Hope Road on the east side and Half Way Tree Road (which changes to Constant Spring Road) on the west, the main thoroughfare through New Kingston is **Hope Road**. Here you'll find the modern convention hotels, restaurants and nightclubs preferred by most visitors.

North of New Kingston lies the city's most beautiful area, **Constant Spring**, which sports magnificent homes. Stunning vistas are found here, especially in the early evening when you can watch the city lights come out.

East of Kingston, the views are even more spectacular, both day and night. Follow Hope Road past the University of the West Indies as it becomes Gordon Town Road and curls its way up into the **Blue Mountains**.

> ◎ **TIP**
>
> Hire a good driver for this stretch of Colorado Rockies-type road: drop-offs are sheer and there are no guardrails!

West of Kingston lies **Spanish Town**. This was once Santiago de la Vega, the island's capital city under Spanish rule. Those early explorers came to Jamaica in search of precious metals and finally gave up the island to the English in 1655. Spanish Town is 12 miles west of Kingston on A-1, and is an excellent day trip for those with an interest in history.

⚠ WARNING

This area is generally safe during weekday business hours, but at 5 pm it takes on the feeling of a ghost town as people head back up into the hills.

Best Places to Stay

Room prices vary greatly with type of accommodation, location and time of year. High season (mid-December through mid-April) brings prices about 40% higher than in summer months.

Money Matters

For accommodations, our price scale is designed to give you a ballpark figure for a typical stay during peak season. We've based these estimates on high season for a standard room for two persons. These prices do not take into account options such as meal plans or dive packages.

Accommodation Price Scale

Prices are given in US dollars.

Deluxe. . . . . $300+
Expensive . . . . $200-$300
Moderate . . . . $100-$200
Inexpensive. . . . . Under $100

All our hotel selections take major credit cards, are air-conditioned and have private baths, except in the case of the few guest houses where noted.

Resorts

THE COURTLEIGH HOTEL AND SUITES
85 Knutsford Boulevard
New Kingston
☎ 876-929-9000, fax 876-926-7744
Moderate

Golf, squash & tennis can be arranged at The Courtleigh.

This 10-story hotel is a new addition in the business district, although the Courtleigh name has been familiar to Kingston visitors for many years. Originally located a short distance from its present site, the family-owned hotel relocated. The 118-room property is aimed at business travelers, but most people will find its rooms comfortable. The hotel includes a restaurant, nightclub and also a fitness center.

CROWNE PLAZA KINGSTON
211 Constant Spring Road
New Kingston
☎ 876-925-7676, fax 876-925-5757
Reservations: ☎ 800-618-6534
Moderate

This fairly new business hotel is perched in the hills just north of New Kingston in the neighborhood of Constant Spring. Many rooms have views of the city and all guests have all the amenities common to Crowne Plazas, such as a fitness center, satellite TV and tennis courts. Guests can enjoy indoor or outdoor dining at Isabella's for a great city view.

HILTON NEW KINGSTON
77 Knutsford Boulevard
New Kingston
☎ 876-926-5430, fax 876-7439
Moderate to Expensive

This hotel was formerly the Wyndham New Kingston and is located in the hotel section of New Kingston near Le Meridien and The Courtleigh. The 303-room property recently underwent a $15 million renovation. It now offers guests many facilities, including a health club, sauna, Olympic-size pool, tennis courts and more.

Guests at the Hilton can use the services of a tennis pro.

LE MERIDIEN JAMAICA PEGASUS
81 Knutsford Boulevard
New Kingston
☎ 876-926-3690, fax 876-929-5855
Moderate

The Pegasus is right in the heart of New Kingston, within walking distance of The Courtleigh and the Wyndham Kingston Hotel. The 17-floor property has 350 guest rooms, each with balcony, satellite TV, hair dryer, safe, two direct dial phones and coffee maker. Upgraded rooms are found on the floors set aside for the Knutsford Club members, with separate check-in, afternoon snacks and upgraded amenities.

The large, deep pool at the Pegasus lies just behind the property and offers a quiet afternoon getaway with scarcely any traffic noise. Tennis courts and jogging trails are also available.

Intimate Inns

STRAWBERRY HILL
New Castle Road
Irishtown
☎ 876-944-8400 or 800/OUTPOST, fax 876-944-8408
www.islandlife.com
Deluxe

This sprawling mountainside resort is perched 3,100 feet above sea level, looking down on Kingston. But the atmosphere here is pure nature. Jamaica's doctor bird, a hummingbird with an unbelievable plume tail, flits through the trees. A morning mist hangs over the mahogany trees. The sound of life in small neighboring villages wafts up from the surrounding valleys.

During our stay at Strawberry Hill, models Kate Moss and Naomi Campbell were also guests.

The resort is one of the Island Outpost properties owned by Chris Blackwell, founder of Island Records, record label of the late Bob Marley (he recuperated at this site after he was shot in 1976), as well as Melissa Manchester and Robert Palmer. Like other Island Outposts, this property is exclusive and unique, drawing many celebrities.

There are 12 wooden villas, each filled with antique Jamaican decor. The villas look out on the Blue Mountains from bedrooms, living rooms and expansive porches. We spent part of our time just lazing about in an oversized hammock on our porch. Every room has electric mattress pads to warm up the bed on chilly evenings, mosquito-netted, four-poster mahogany beds, stocked kitchenettes, coffee makers, televisions, VCRs and even CD players with a full array of CDs (okay, some of them are Island Record productions, but they fit the tone of the place.) Videos are available for loan.

In January 1998, Strawberry Hill opened a new Aveda Spa, with massage, hydrotherapy, facials and other body treatments. We enjoyed pedicures, manicures and a splendid facial. And, at the end of the day, guests can enjoy a spa cuisine or Jamaican dishes with a light touch in the resort restaurant.

TERRA NOVA
17 Waterloo Road
New Kingston
☎ 876-926-9334, fax 876-929-4933
www.cariboutpost.com/terra_nova
Moderate

Terra Nova is New Kingston at its very best: formal, traditional and oh-so Jamaican. Unlike the modern highrises also found in this business district, Terra Nova carries on the legacy of Old Jamaica with classic mahogany furniture, fine art and a wonderful atmosphere that tells you you're not staying in another chain hotel.

There are only 35 guest rooms at this intimate property, which is a favorite with those who have been coming to Kingston for many years.

⭐ **DID YOU KNOW?**

Terra Nova was originally a colonial mansion, the family home of Chris Blackwell many years ago.

Best Places to Eat

Money Matters

Our dining price scale is based on a three-course dinner, including appetizer or soup, an entrée, dessert and coffee. Cocktails and wine are extra.

Dining Price Scale

Prices are per person in US dollars.

Expensive. . . . . $40+ per person
Moderate . . . . $25-$40
Inexpensive. . . . . Under $25

Fine Dining

BLUE MOUNTAIN INN
Gordon Town Road
☎ 876-927-1700 or 876-927-2606
Expensive

Save the Blue Mountain Inn for your best night out.

Jackets are required.

Reservations are required for this beautiful eatery located half an hour out of Kingston in the misty Blue Mountains, tucked behind a bougainvillea-draped entrance. The menu features beef and seafood, all served in a classic English-inn atmosphere. White-glove service makes this a truly elegant evening. The restaurant is open for dinner only.

TIP

We recommend this often-lauded eatery for those seeking a romantic evening that combines the talents of a professional chef with the bounty of Jamaica.

EL DORADO RESTAURANT
Terra Nova Hotel
17 Waterloo Road
New Kingston
☎ 876-926-9334 or 876-926-2211
Moderate to Expensive

El Dorado is the fine dining restaurant at Terra Nova, known for its seafood dishes as well as steaks. The air-conditioned restaurant is a favorite meeting place for the power lunch crowd and is open noon to 2:30 for lunch and 7 to 11 pm for dinner.

GROG SHOPPE
Devon House
26 Hope Road
New Kingston
☎ 876-929-7027
Inexpensive to Moderate

This excellent restaurant offers both indoor and open-air seating in a pub-like setting. Just steps from Devon House itself, the restaurant offers a menu that ranges from pub lunches such as roast beef or corned tongue to escovitch fish and steam fish in white wine, onions, tomatoes and herbs. Many Jamaican specialties are offered, including curried goat, ackee and saltfish, roast suckling pig, baked crab backs, curried chicken, jerked chicken and stuffed cho-cho.

IVOR GUEST HOUSE
Jack's Hill
☎ 876-978-3476 or 876-978-3479
Moderate to Expensive

When you're ready for a break from continental or Jamaican food, this elegant restaurant serves up Cantonese and Thai delights. Don't miss the dim sum on Sunday afternoons.

LA FRESCA BAR AND GRILL
Terra Nova Hotel
17 Waterloo Road
New Kingston
☎ 876-926-9334 or 876-926-2211
Expensive

We enjoyed an elegant dinner at La Fresca just days before Christmas one year. It was on our last night in Jamaica, and we dined outside on the great house verandah. Local residents, decked in their holiday splendor, filled most tables. The restaurant and the hotel were lit by tiny white lights and the diner was one we'll never forget.

Menu selections are mostly from the sea and include: peppered shrimp, grilled lobster tail, fish escovitch, fish soup, conch fritters and fried fish.

ORCHID ROOM
Devon House
26 Hope Road
New Kingston
☎ 876-968-2098
Moderate

This dinner-only restaurant serves authentic Thai cuisine. Pad Thai, pepper steak, curried dishes, stir fried chicken and satay fill the menu.

STRAWBERRY HILL
New Castle Road
Irishtown
☎ 876-944-8400
Moderate to Expensive

The open-air restaurant at Strawberry Hill serves a continental breakfast daily followed by lunch and dinner featuring "new Jamaican cuisine." These innovative dishes are the creation of Jamaican-born Chef James Palmer. The Sunday brunch is a Kingston event; look for diners in their Sunday bests at this popular happening.

Menu selections include: blackened sirloin steak with red onion marmalade; grilled jumbo shrimp brushed with rum molasses; and grilled chicken breast with roasted corn.

Strawberry Hill also offers a spa menu. Items such as grilled yellowtail snapper with mushroom tomato broth and free-range grilled chicken breast on a bed of steamed callaloo with peanut wine sauce liven the palate without adding unnecessary calories or fat. We recommend this restaurant both for its spectacular view and for its innovative cuisine featuring Jamaican dishes with a culinary twist.

Informal Dining

HOT POT
2 Alamont Terrace
Kingston
☎ 876-929-3906
Inexpensive to Moderate

This favorite local hangout serves three meals a day: Jamaican favorites such as ackee and codfish, rundown and escovitch fish. Wash it all down with fresh juices such as tamarind, coconut water and, if you visit during the holiday season, sorrel.

This popular place offers a real taste of Jamaican food and a genuine Jamaican atmosphere to match.

I SCREAM
Devon House
26 Hope Road
New Kingston
Inexpensive

We normally wouldn't put an ice cream parlor in a restaurant section, but I Scream doesn't serve up your typical dairy dessert. You can find grapenut, guava, mango, soursop and even Devon stout ice creams. Need we say more?

PEPPERS
31 Upper Waterloo Road
Kingston
☎ 876-969-2421
Inexpensive to Moderate

Want to feel like a Kingstonian? Then do as the locals do and head to this casual restaurant, grab a picnic table, and order up some jerk and a Red Stripe.

The restaurant is an open-air affair, completely casual. Specialties of the house include jerk chicken, jerk pork and jerk fish. Garlic crab and grilled lobster are other favorites.

There are two bars here, as well as a dance floor. The site is a popular after-work place for Kingstonians, who come on Wednesday and Friday nights for seafood, Tuesday for wine and cheese accompanied by live country music, karaoke on Thursdays, and oldies tunes on Sunday evenings.

All entrées come with a tasty soup at Peppers.

Like the Hot Pot, we recommend this casual eatery for a real taste of Jamaican food and a real Jamaican atmosphere.

Sunup To Sundown

Kingston is a good destination if you're looking for activity away from the beach. Although there are some good beaches in the Kingston area (see below), the city is really noted for its arts and cultural scene, as well as historic attractions.

Beaches

Kingston's beaches are busy. There have been some crime problems on them in recent years, so we recommend exercising caution.

The Hellshire area, southwest of the city, has some of the best-known area beaches, including **Gunboat Beach** and **Fort Clarence**. **Lime Cay**, south of the peninsula where Port Royal and the airport are located, can be reached by a boat from Morgan's Harbor and is very popular with swimmers as well as picnickers looking for a nice day trip out of the city.

Don't take any valuables to the beach with you!

Golf

You have two choices for golf in the Kingston area.

CAYMANAS GOLF CLUB
☎ 876-922-3386

Caymanas was Jamaica's first major championship 18-hole course, dating from the 1950s. It was designed by Howard Watson and is located six miles west of Kingston. A round of golf costs $53; rentals are available. Facilities include a snack bar, carts and a pro shop.

CONSTANT SPRING
☎ 876-924-1610

The Constant Spring course is an easy choice for business travelers who don't have time to drive to Caymanas.

This downtown course dates back to 1920 when it was designed by Scotsman Stanley Thompson, the mentor of Robert Trent Jones. The short course is a par 70, and a round costs $35; rentals are available. There's a clubhouse, restaurant, bar and pro shop.

Tennis

Tennis players can test their skills at several courts, including the **Crowne Plaza** (☎ 876-925-7676), **LeMeridien Pegasus** (☎ 876-926-3690), and the **Hilton New Kingston** (☎ 876-926-5430).

Sights & Attractions

BOB MARLEY MUSEUM
56 Hope Road
Kingston
☎ 876-927-9152
Hours: 9 am - 5 pm, Monday, Tuesday, Thursday and Friday; 12:30 - 5 pm, Wednesday and Saturday
Admission

Marley fans shouldn't miss this shrine to the legendary reggae superstar, housed in the musician's home. A visit here includes a tour and a movie about Marley's life.

CAYMANAS PARK RACE TRACK
Gregory Park
☎ 876-988-2523

The track is a favorite with locals and visitors who get their kicks from exciting horse races. Races are held on Wednesdays, Saturdays and on public holidays, 12:30 to 6 pm.

DEVON HOUSE
26 Hope Road
New Kingston
☎ 876-929-6602
Hours: 9 am - 5 pm, Tuesday through Saturday
Admission

This restored great house is set in the heart of
New Kingston, near the Terra Nova Hotel. The
home was built in 1889 for 10,000 pounds by a
Venezuelan gold millionaire. The family lived in
the home until the 1920s. Today, the historic
structure is filled with antiques and antique reproductions from the 1880s (done by Things Jamaican). Tours, given every 15 minutes, include a
look at the master bedroom, the sewing room with
an illegal gambling room upstairs (the stairs are
hidden in the ceiling), a sunny ballroom with relief ceiling, original chandelier and an English piano.

GUARDSMAN'S "SERENITY" FISHING
& WILDLIFE SANCTUARY
40 minutes east of Kingston via A1/A2 west.
Open daily
Admission

A popular new stop with Kingston school groups,
this sanctuary was established by the executive
chairman of the Guardsman Group, a security
company in Kingston. A visit to the site starts
with a tractor ride through mango orchards and
vegetable plots, then a visit to the animal collection, with exotic birds and a petting zoo.

Food lovers will be interested in the sanctuary for
another reason: local dishes are served for lunch
and dinner by the restaurant. Curried goat, bar-

becue or jerked chicken, oxtail and other local dishes are available for $8-$10.

You can even fish for red tilapia and have the restaurant clean and bag your catch for $4 per pound.

HOPE BOTANICAL GARDENS AND ZOO
Hope Road, next to the University of the West Indies Mona campus.
☎ 876-927-1257
Open daily
Admission

This 50-acre getaway is the largest botanical garden in the West Indies. The small zoo features Caribbean wildlife.

NATIONAL ART GALLERY
Roy West Building
Kingston Mall
☎ 876-922-8540
Hours: 11 - 4:30 weekdays only
Admission

This downtown art gallery contains some real treasures. The best-known artists represented here are Edna Manley (an accomplished artist and wife of the former prime minister, Norman Manley) and Kapo, whose religious images have received a lot of attention.

WORLD'S END LTD.
Gordon Town
Hours: 10 am - 4 pm, Monday through Friday; 12 - 4 pm, Saturday and Saturday
☎ 876-977-5941 or 929-3564

Even non rum-drinkers will find this tour worth-while, thanks to the beautiful location. World's End produces Sangster's Old Jamaican Liqueurs high in the Blue Mountains. Tours of the factory are followed by a taste of the potent and well-respected product.

⊙ TIP

Birders shouldn't miss World's End. Bring your binoculars for the chance to see the Doctor Bird, Jamaica's national bird.

Shop Till You Drop

 Because it does have far fewer tourists than the resort areas, Kingston shopping is primarily aimed at residents. One area that tourists will find of interest, however, is **Devon House**. Surrounding the great house are numerous boutiques offering everything from Jamaican artwork to jerk sauces.

Things Jamaican is one of the best stores for those looking to take back a taste of Jamaica. This shop sells sauces, cookbooks and even pewterware that reproduces patterns recovered by archaeologists at Port Royal. A second Things Jamaican shop is located at Norman Manley International Airport.

Pick up some last-minute coffee supplies at **The Coffee Mill**, which also sells teas and sauces.

Two Hampers and a Mule is another excellent stop and offers local artwork, cookbooks and more.

Fine Jewelry

BIJOUX JEWELERS
Norman Manley International Airport
☎ 876-924-8114

Like its cousins in Montego Bay, this shop sells gold jewelry and fine watches.

Watches

SWISS STORES
Mall Plaza
20 Constant Spring Road
☎ 876-926-6537

SWISS STORES
Le Meridien Jamaica Pegasus
☎ 876-929-8147

After Dark

Kingston nightlife is legendary, starting with "Friday Night Jam." This open-air street party begins when folks leave work on Friday night and people go out into the street to buy the evening meal, to sit with friends, and to take it easy. Ask for suggestions from your hotel staff before you head out on the town for the evening.

Discos

There are several well-known discos in Kingston.

MIRAGE
106 Hope Road
Sovereign Centre
☎ 876-978-8557

PEPPERS
31 Upper Waterloo Road
☎ 876-925-2219

Kingston A-Z

Banks

Bank of Nova Scotia
35 King Street, Kingston
☎ 876-922-1420

Citizens Bank
4 King Street, Kingston
☎ 876-922-5850

Currency Exchange

Most of Kingston's larger hotels offer currency exchange, usually at a rate slightly lower than the bank rate. You can also make currency exchange at the banks or at:

FX Trader
20 Tobago Avenue
☎ 888-FX-TRADER

Cambioman
7 Holborn Road
☎ 876-960-6699

Embassies

US Embassy
2 Oxford Road, Kingston
☎ 876-929-4850 or 920-9565

Canadian High Commission
30 Knutsford Boulevard, Kingston
☎ 876-926-1500

British High Commission
Trafalgar Road, Kingston
☎ 876-926-9050

Japanese Embassy
32 Trafalgar Road, Kingston
☎ 876-929-3389

**Embassy of the Federal
Republic of Germany**
10 Waterloo Road, Kingston
☎ 876-926-6728

French Embassy
13 Hillcrest Avenue, Kingston
☎ 876-978-1297

Emergency Phone Numbers

Ambulance 110
Police. 119
Fire 110

Hospital

University Hospital
Mona, Kingston
☎ 876-927-1620

Optical Services

Superior Optical
28 Constant Spring Road
☎ 876-926-5024

Supreme Optical Co. Ltd.
Brentford Mall
39 Brentford Road
☎ 876-968-3491

Broadbent Jamaica Ltd.
1 Duke Street
☎ 876-922-4721

Broadbent Jamaica Ltd.
Nuttail Medical Centre
Cross Road
☎ 876-926-7572

South Coast

Introduction

Vacationers to Jamaica are happy to hear "no problem" as an answer to just about any request – whether it's for another Red Stripe beer or a taxi or more towels in the room.

But if travelers cruising the South Coast hear "crocodiles, no problem" when confronting a seven-foot specimen, some seem a little incredulous. Others, looking at the toothy reptile just yards from the boat, get downright worried. But there's no need to fear; these crocodiles represent no threat. Unlike their cousins on the Nile, the *Americanus crocodilius* is not aggressive. Like vacationers on the nearby beach in Negril, they're content to lie in the sun and take life easy.

Crocodiles can be seen on the Black River, just one attraction along Jamaica's little developed South Coast. This is a destination where visitors have the chance to see the natural side of Jamaica, where smoke rises, not from ganja, but from spontaneous combustion fires in the dense peat bogs.

The **Black River**, at 44 miles the longest river in Jamaica, is named for the color of its water that comes from the peat bog runoff. The water on the lower stretch is also brackish, as salt water comes in and mixes with the fresh water during high tide. These conditions are perfect for mangroves, which have roots that cascade from high branches and reach the water. The result is a curtain of thick roots, an almost impenetrable fence that divides the river from the marshy swampland beyond the trees.

Fishermen use wire traps to catch blue Marie crabs. Shrimp are caught using the shrimp trap, an African design dating back over 400 years.

The Shrimp Trap

The bamboo trap, shaped like a large inverted bottle, holds coconut and oranges in the wide end. After two or three days in the river, the trap is checked and the shrimp fall out when the smaller end is twisted (much like pouring liquid from a bottle).

⊚ TIP

In the St. Elizabeth parish, look for women on the side of the road selling bags of peppered shrimp. Highly salted and spiced, these small shrimp are a popular snack with locals and visitors.

The waters are also dotted with bull rush, giant ferns (one of 600 species found in this country) and pancake lilies. Your captain will probably point out things of interest, such as a 35-year-old termite nest and trees where over 3,000 cattle egrets nest nightly.

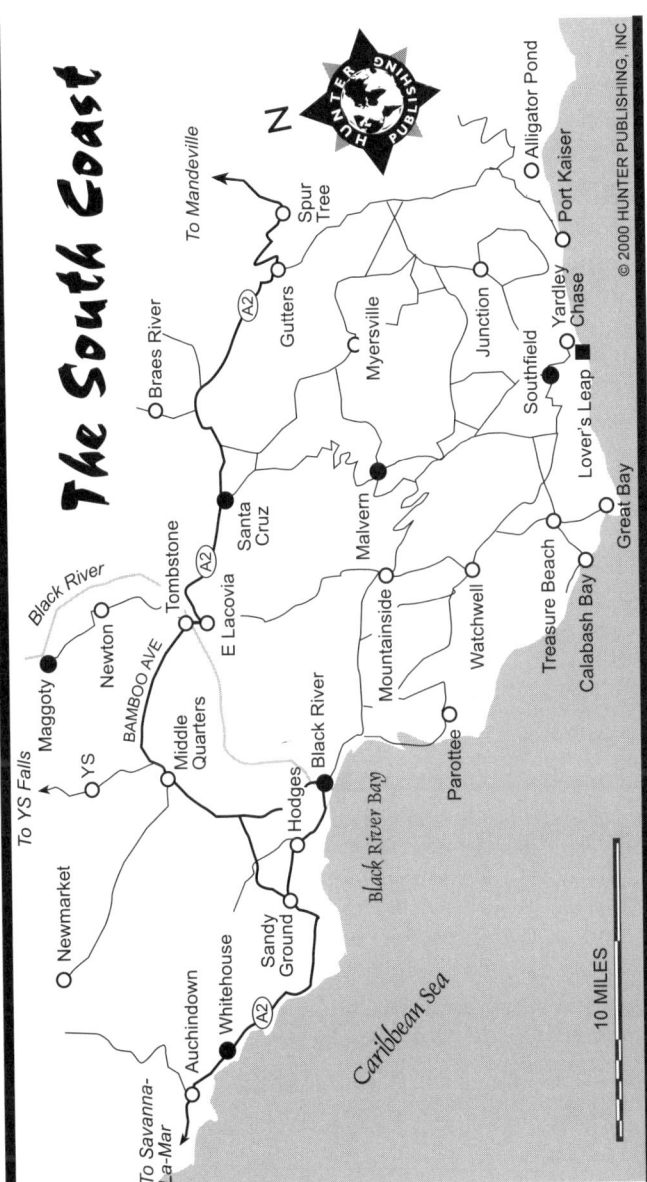

The South Coast

South Coast

But the biggest attraction on the Black River are the crocodiles. Once hunted, these crocodiles are now protected but still remain wary of humans. Loud talk (or even a spear fisherman at work) causes the crocodile to take refuge.

Beyond Black River, the main road winds through numerous small towns and inland villages. One especially notable stretch is called **Bamboo Avenue**. This scenic drive winds for over two miles, a green tunnel of tall bamboo that arches over the roadway. Along Bamboo Avenue, vendors sell chilled young coconuts, cracking them with a quick machete chop to reveal the jelly inside.

The road finally twists and turns its way to the city of **Mandeville**. Here sun, sand and surf give way to a Jamaica untouched by expansive resorts, limbo contests or duty-free shops. Located in the shadow of the Don Figuero Mountains, this dignified, proper city is rarely seen by tourists.

Mandeville is perched at an elevation of 2,000 feet above sea level, ensuring cooler days and nights than found along the island's coast. The region first appealed to Jamaica's English settlers, who came here to escape the heat and founded a town in 1816. Soon an English-style community took shape, complete with a central square and clock tower. Small hotels arose to serve the expatriates and travelers who came to do business in the area's bauxite industry.

But in the 1950s, Jamaica's other assets, its beautiful beaches and coastal areas, began to outshine this getaway. Tourism in Mandeville declined, although the area became a favorite with Jamaicans who had lived abroad and returned to retire, building truly grand homes.

Today, Mandeville is a strong contrast to other Jamaican cities. Shiny new fast food outlets stand on clean, guttered streets. Jamaica's omnipresent burglar bars are missing from many residences. Massive homes, as impressive as any along the California coastline, cling to hillsides. No vendors search for travelers.

After a look around town, it's easy to see that Mandeville boasts the highest standard of living on the island as well as the lowest crime rate.

★ DID YOU KNOW?

Much of the wealth seen in Mandeville comes from Alcan's Jamaica bauxite plant, the region's major employer.

Throughout Jamaica it's common to see pedestrians, but in Mandeville these walkers stroll, not just to the market or to a hotel job, but on their morning constitutional. Many choose to stay fit at the **Manchester Club**, the oldest golf course in the Caribbean. This nine-hole course is set on rolling hills. Nearby tennis courts challenge players and indoor squash courts offer more fast action.

Other activities in Mandeville include a tour of the **High Mountain Coffee Factory**. Jamaica's second best-known variety after Blue Mountain, this coffee originates on nearby plantations and is produced here at the factory. Tours can be ar-

South Coast

ranged and a sample taste of the island's java awaits at the gift shop.

> ★ **DID YOU KNOW?**
>
> Of the 25 bird species endemic to Jamaica, all but two are found in the Mandeville region.

Nature lovers also flock to Mandeville. Gardening buffs find numerous gardens filled with orchids as well as a fruit that was developed in Mandeville: the ortanique. The combination orange and tangerine is unique, hence the name.

 # Getting There

There is no commercial airport in Mandeville. Travelers usually arrive in Kingston and make the two-hour drive to Mandeville.

> ⚠ **WARNING**
>
> Driving in Jamaica is challenging (to say the least), with winding roads, daredevil drivers and innumerable pedestrians and livestock, outnumbered only by potholes.

Driving is on the left. Most travelers arrange for taxi transport.

Mandeville

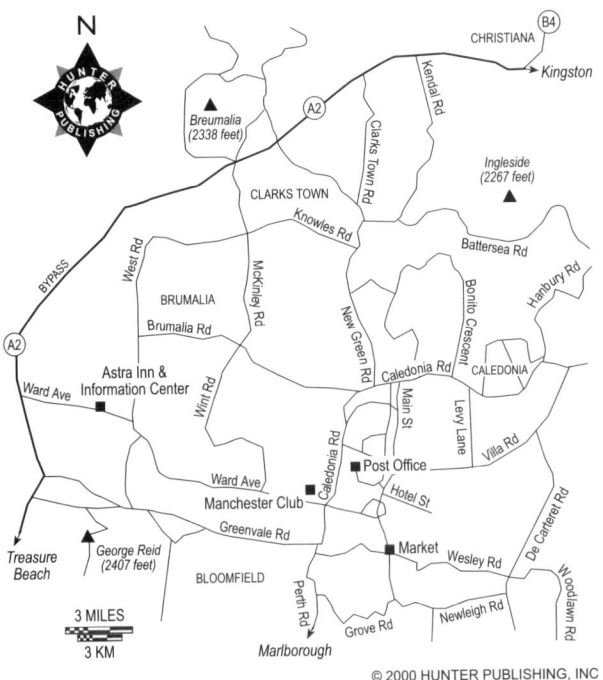

Breumalia (2338 feet)

CHRISTIANA B4

→ Kingston

Ingleside (2267 feet)

CLARKS TOWN

BRUMALIA

Astra Inn & Information Center

Manchester Club

BLOOMFIELD

Treasure Beach

George Reid (2407 feet)

CALEDONIA

Post Office

Market

Marlborough

3 MILES
3 KM

© 2000 HUNTER PUBLISHING, INC

South Coast

Getting Around

Car & Jeep Rentals

Away from the main tourist areas, you'll find that rental cars are fewer in this region of Jamaica. Some companies can be found in Mandeville.

SOUTH COAST CAR RENTAL AGENCIES	
Maxdan Car Rentals and Tours	☎ 876-962-5341 (6 North Race Course Road)
Millinex Rentals	☎ 876-962-3542 (3 Villa Road)
Moon Glow Car Rental	☎ 876-962-9097 (3 Caledonia Road)

Best Places to Stay

Money Matters

Room prices vary greatly with type of accommodation, location, and time of year. High season (mid-December through mid-April) brings prices about 40% higher than in summer months. Because Mandeville and Black River are removed from the tourist scene, you will note that prices are markedly lower than on the North Coast.

Treasure Beach is developing a tourist following, so prices there are more in keeping with other resort areas.

We've based these estimates on high season (December 15-April 15) for a standard room for two persons. These prices do not take into account options, such as meal plans and dive packages.

Accommodations Price Scale

Prices are given in US dollars.

Deluxe . . . . $300+
Expensive . . . . $200-$300
Moderate . . . . $100-$200
Inexpensive . . . . Under $100

★ NOTE

Along the South Coast, stores, restaurants and accommodations mark their prices in Jamaican dollars. As we have been using US dollars to denote prices throughout this book, we will continue to do so here. Use the chart on page 99 for conversions.

Resorts

MANDEVILLE HOTEL
4 Hotel Street
Box 78
Mandeville
☎ 876-962-2460, fax 876-962-0700
Inexpensive

The Mandeville offers a delightful blend of traditional Jamaican elegance and modern comfort and convenience. Just steps from the downtown square, the hotel sits on the site of one of Mandeville's first buildings, a structure used as an officers' quarters and mess in a former "hill

The Mandeville is our favorite.

South Coast

station." In 1875 the site became the Waverley Hotel, later changing to the Brooks Hotel before finally becoming the Mandeville Hotel. It's operated by Ceceline McIntyre, and has a warm and charming atmosphere. There are 46 units, including 17 housekeeping suites with one, two or three bedrooms. The hotel has a nice pool adjacent to the restaurant.

Intimate Inns

THE ASTRA COUNTRY INN
AND RESTAURANT
62 Ward Avenue, Box 60
☎ 876-962-7979 or 962-3725, fax 876-962-1461
Inexpensive

Astra offers 20 guest rooms, each with air-conditioning and some with kitchenettes. We enjoyed a stay in the housekeeping suite, complete with bedroom, living room with convertible couch, and full kitchen. This isn't the suite of a North Coast resort, but for the money and hospitality here, it can't be beat.

FLEUR FLATS RESORTS
10 Coke Drive, PO Box 485
☎ 876-962-1053, fax 876-905-3429
Inexpensive

There's nothing fancy about Fleur Flats, but if you're interested in an extended stay in the Mandeville area, this is a good choice. The furnished two-bedroom apartments come with the comforts of home and maid service is available.

HOTEL VILLA BELLA
Christiana
☎ 876-964-2243, fax 876-964-2765
Inexpensive

This bed and breakfast is in the community of Christiana, 13 miles from Mandeville. Perched at 3,000 feet above sea level, it has the feel of a country inn. There are 18 rooms in the two-story inn, which also includes six acres of gardens, a reading room, television lounge, the Nasturtium Room restaurant, cocktail lounge, outdoor garden terrace, gift shop, and, on request, high tea.

INVERCAULD GREAT HOUSE AND HOTEL
Black River
☎ 876-965-2750 or 968-1053, fax 876-965-2751
Inexpensive

This hotel offers 52 air-conditioned rooms and suites with private bathrooms and balconies. This great house was built over a century ago by a Scottish businessman, and only recently became a hotel. Dr. Trevor Hamilton, an international businessman born in the area, converted the home into a hotel for visitors looking to enjoy the South Coast. Amenities include a restaurant, cocktail bar, swimming pool, tennis, disco, gift shop and tour desk.

The Invercauld is just a short walk from the sea or from the center of Black River.

JAKE'S VILLAGE
Treasure Beach
☎ 876-965-0635
Reservations: ☎ 800/OUTPOST
www.islandlife.com
Moderate to Deluxe

Jake's is a unique property, a place for those really looking to get away from it all and into a relaxed rhythm with the sea. Beach kitsch best describes the decor of the resort's eight guest units, each in pale shades of ochre, blue, pink and lavender with tin roofs. Five single cottages and two two-bedroom cottages make up the offerings, along with Abalone, a two-story, three-bedroom guest villa built in the style of a miniature Moroccan palace with terra-cotta walls.

Each of the guest rooms at Jake's is filled with rustic local furniture: cast iron beds and platform beds covered with a veil of mosquito netting. Each room includes a private bathroom and outdoor shower. Rooms are not air-conditioned, but each includes a ceiling fan.

TREASURE BEACH HOTEL
Treasure Beach
☎ 876-965-0110, fax 876-965-2544
Reservations: ☎ 800/742-4276
Moderate

This quiet hotel offers air-conditioned rooms right on the beach. It's also home to the Yabba Restaurant and near many attractions, such as Lovers Leap. Each of the rooms has a ceiling fan and private verandah. A pool is set in a grove of tall coconut palms.

Best Places to Eat

Money Matters

For dining, we've set up a price scale based on a three-course dinner including appetizer or soup, an entrée, dessert and coffee. Cocktails and wine are extra.

Dining Price Scale

Prices are per person in US dollars.

Expensive. . . . . $40+ per person
Moderate . . . . $25-$40
Inexpensive. . . . . Under $25

Recommended Restaurants

BLOOMFIELD GREAT HOUSE
8 Perth Road
☎ 876-962-7130, 962-7192
Moderate to Expensive

International-Caribbean cuisine is the order of the day at Mandeville's finest restaurant. Once Bill Laurie's Steakhouse, this location has re-opened and undergone an elegant refurbishment. Guests can dine on an open-air verandah, which offers a spectacular view of the Mandeville lights at night, or inside in the antiques-filled main dining room. Don't miss the bar, which is open daily and affords a great view of the city. It's an all-

Bloomfield has a private dining room for quiet evenings alone or for families.

wood affair reminiscent of a century-old pub and Australian and Chilean wines are featured.

Entrées include: filet mignon with roasted garlic guava sauce; beef Wellington; seafood kebob; shrimp Creole; and grilled pork chops stuffed with tropical fruits and served with plum sauce.

THE ASTRA COUNTRY INN AND RESTAURANT
62 Ward Avenue
☎ 876-962-7979 or 962-3725
Moderate

The restaurant is just past the inn's lobby. Like the hotel itself, it's clean and simple. But there's nothing simple about the food here: these are traditional Jamaican dishes such as jerk chicken, salad with peanut dressing, and an unbeatable rice and peas.

JAKE'S VILLAGE
Treasure Beach
☎ 876-965-0635
Moderate to Expensive

Jake's Village is one of the best known spots on the South Coast.

Jake's is an open-air restaurant serving Jamaican cuisine such as ackee and saltfish, conch salad, pumpkin soup and steamed fresh.

THE MANCHESTER ARMS PUB AND RESTAURANT
Mandeville Hotel
4 Hotel Street
☎ 876-962-2460
Moderate

Resembling a traditional English pub, this dark, cool place is an excellent spot to meet other travelers and enjoy a cool beer. When you're ready for a meal, dine on Jamaican specialties.

MANDEVILLE HOTEL
4 Hotel Street
☎ 876-962-2460
Moderate

Good, traditional Jamaican dishes are the order of the day at this inn just off the central square.

THE NASTURTIUM ROOM
Hotel Villa Bella
Christiana
☎ 876-964-2243
Moderate to Expensive

The Nasturtium Room is open 7 am to 10 pm daily and features a variety of dishes, including chicken Szhechuan, chicken marengo in pineapple sauce, lobster fettucine, shrimp Creole, T-bone steak, and more.

YABBA RESTAURANT
Treasure Beach Hotel
Treasure Beach
☎ 876-965-0110
Moderate

Yabba offers Jamaican cuisine, including fish and lobster, steaks, jerk chicken and lamb.

Many dishes at Yabba incorporate citrus & vegetables grown on the property.

South Coast

Sunup To Sundown

The South Coast of Jamaica has long been synonymous with scuba diving, but this destination also presents plenty of other types of fun in the sun. However you may define soft adventure – walking, birding, golf, hiking, snorkeling, bicycling, fishing, or horseback riding – you'll find it here, complete with professional instruction and rental facilities.

Beaches

Treasure Beach is the best known stretch of sand on the South Coast. Folks comenot only for the beach, but also to visit Jake's.

Golf

MANCHESTER COUNTRY CLUB
☎ 876-962-2403

This golf club is home to the oldest course in Jamaica and one of the oldest in the entire Caribbean. At an elevation of over 2,000 feet above sea level, it enjoys much cooler temperatures than the courses found along the coast. There are nine greens and 18 tee boxes.

Tennis

MANCHESTER COUNTRY CLUB
☎ 876-962-2403

The country club opens its tennis courts to visitors of the many small properties in the area that don't have their own facilities.

Unique Tours

MARVELOUS MANDEVILLE TOUR
☎ 876-962-3725, 876-962-3265 or 800/JAMAICA
Fax: 876-962-1461
Tours by reservation only
Admission

A Marvelous Mandeville Tour (US $40) includes a welcome get-together at a local home, tour of Mandeville, shopping, lunch and high tea. The tour is operated by Diana McIntyre, owner of the Astra Country Inn and Restaurant.

BAMMY FACTORY
Mandeville
☎ 876-962-3725 or 962-3265
Hours: Open Tuesday and Wednesday only

Bammy is a staple in the Jamaican diet, a delicacy made from the cassava root that dates back to the days of the Arawak Indians. Tours of the Bammy Factory, housed in Mr. Clem Bloomfield's home, are given on Tuesdays and Wednesdays. Contact your hotel desk or call Countrystyle at ☎ 876-962-3725 or 876-962-3265, fax 876-962-1461 or 800/JAMAICA. (The Countrystyle tour company is the only one that organizes these trips.)

PICKAPEPPA SAUCE FACTORY TOUR
Shooter's Hill
☎ 876-962-2928
Tours by appointment only
Admission

Near Mandeville, Shooter's Hill is the home to one of Jamaica's best known (and one of our best loved) exports: Pickapeppa Sauce. It is used by cooks to spice up eggs, meats and sauces, and is a mix of tamarind, onions, tomatoes, sugar, cane vinegar, mangoes, raisins and other spices. Pickapeppa Sauce is prepared in this small, nondescript factory. Tours aren't scheduled, but if you're interested, call Countrystyle (☎ 876-962-3725 or 962-3265) to see if they can help you get a look at this fragrant operation.

Nature Tours

BLACK RIVER SAFARI CRUISE
Black River
☎ 876-965-2513
Open daily
Admission

At 44 miles, the Black River is the longest in Jamaica.

This is a popular day trip that takes travelers up the Black River. The waters here contain snook and tarpon, some reaching as large as 200 pounds. You may see spear fishermen with a snorkel, mask and speargun, swimming in the dark water stained by peat deposits. Among their catch are tiny brine shrimp, sold by women in the St. Elizabeth parish along the roadside. Highly salted and spiced, the shrimp are a popular snack with locals and visitors.

South Coast

★ **DID YOU KNOW?**

The fisherman's canoes are hand-hewn and burned out using a generations-old technique.

The biggest attraction on the Black River are the crocodiles. This protected species can live as long as 100 years, and some of the old-timers have become known by local residents. One 15-foot-long croc named Lester is seen nightly.

JACANA AQUA TOURS LTD.
Black River
☎ 876-965-2513
Hours: 8:30 am - 5 pm daily
Admission

Jacana offers a safari boat tour on the Black River. Package includes trip to Y.S. Falls.

MRS. STEPHENSON'S GARDEN
☎ 876-962-3725 or 876-962-3265,
fax 876-962-1461 or 800/JAMAICA
Mandeville
Open by appointment only
Admission

Mrs. Stephenson has won many prizes from the Mandeville Horticulture Society (the oldest such group in North America). Her gardens are filled with orchids as well as a fruit that was developed in Mandeville: the ortanique.

Mrs. Stephenson's Garden is open by reservation only.

Ortanique

Mandeville is where the ortanique was developed. This citrus fruit combines orange and tangerine for a "unique" fruit that's seedless and juicy.

SOUTH COAST SAFARI LTD.
Black River
☎ 876-965-2513
Tour times: 9 and 11 am, 12:30, 2 and 4 pm daily
Admission

This excellent tour company offers a boat tour up the Black River for a chance to see crocodiles as well as rural life and also an excursion to the remote Y.S. Falls.

ST. ELIZABETH SAFARIS
Black River
☎ 876-965-2374
Hours: 8:30 am - 5 pm daily
Admission

Tours of the Black River and Y.S. Falls are available from this large operator. River trips leave daily at 9, 11, 2 and 3:30; Y.S. tours leave every half-hour from 9 to 3:30.

Sights & Attractions

APPLETON ESTATE
Jamaica Estate Tours, ☎ 876-963-9215
or 876-963-9508, fax 876-963-9218 or check
with your hotel's tour desk
Hours: 9 am - 3:30 pm daily, except Sundays
Admission

Sugar cane is a major agricultural product in this
region and for nearly two and a half centuries the
Appleton Estate has produced one of the island's
top exports made from it. Take a tour of the rum
distillery Monday through Saturday. Visitors receive a complimentary bottle at the end of the
Appleton tour.

BAMBOO AVENUE
On A2 between Lacovia and Middle Quarters
Hours: Anytime
Free

Beyond Mandeville's borders, the road west (A2)
winds along one of Jamaica's most scenic
stretches, with a green tunnel of tall bamboo that
arches over the roadway. Along the road's edge,
vendors sell chilled young coconuts (jelly coconuts), cracking them with a quick machete chop
to reveal the jelly inside.

HIGH MOUNTAIN COFFEE FACTORY
☎ 876-963-4211
Open Monday through Friday
Admission

This coffee originates on nearby plantations and
is produced here at the factory. Tours can be ar-

*High Mountain
is Jamaica's
second best-
known variety
after Blue Moun-
tain.*

South Coast

ranged and guests can stop by the gift shop for a sample taste.

LOVERS LEAP
East of Treasure Beach off the main road
Hours: 9 am - 6 pm, Monday through Thursday;
9 am - 7 pm Friday, Saturday and Sunday
☎ 876-965-6634
Admission

This sheer 1,700-foot cliff drops straight into the sea and provides a beautiful view of the coastline. It is a favorite stop with travelers, who enjoy a drink at the Toby Bar (try the "lovers' punch") or dine at the Chardley Restaurant. Tours of local cacti are available, and a miniature farm demonstrates the dry farming technique used in this area.

★ DID YOU KNOW?

Legend has it that from this cliff a pair of lovers, escaped slaves, leapt to their deaths rather than face capture.

MARSHALL'S PEN
Mandeville
☎ 876-963-8569 or 904-5454
Open daily
Admission

Nature lovers flock to Mandeville, and a top birding spot is Marshall's Pen, operated by ornithologist Robert Sutton. Tours are conducted by Sutton and are by appointment only. Nearly 100 species have been recorded at this cattle farm and great houses. This birding site is open by reservation only.

★ **DID YOU KNOW?**

Of the 25 bird species endemic to Jamaica, all but two are found in the Marshall's Pen area.

MILK RIVER MINERAL SPA
Milk River at Clarendon
☎ 876-924-9544
Hours: 7 am - 7 pm daily
Admission

Located 22 miles from Mandeville, these spas offer a soak in natural waters whose high levels of radioactivity soothe aches and pains.

Y.S. FALLS
☎ 876-997-6055
Open daily
Admission

Negril vacationers looking to get away from the sunloving crowds for a while can take a day trip to Y.S. Falls, down along the South Coast. These spectacular waterfalls cascade in steps through tropical forest. As spectacular (and far less crowded) as Dunn's River Falls, Y.S. is a Jamaican attraction that has remained untouched by hassling vendors and long lines. At the top, swimmers enjoy clear waters under a canopy of ferns.

 # South Coast A-Z

Banks

Bank of Nova Scotia
Ward Avenue and Caledonia Road
☎ 876-962-2842

Workers Bank
13 Mandeville Plaza
☎ 876-962-3295

Currency Exchange

Brumalia Hardware
2 Parth Road
☎ 876-962-2115

FX Trader
2 Manch Road
☎ 876-961-1844

Mandeville Cambio
18 West Park Crescent
☎ 876-962-8214

Shields Cambio
Brumalia and Caledonia Roads
☎ 876-962-1935

Emergency Phone Numbers

Ambulance 110
Police. 119
Fire 110

Hospital

Mandeville Hospital
32 Hargreaves Avenue
☎ 876-962-2067

Black River Hospital
45 High Street
☎ 876-965-2212

Pharmacies

Fontana Pharmacy
Manchester Shopping Center
☎ 876-962-3129

Super Plus Shopping Center
☎ 876-961-3007

Hargreaves Pharmacy
32 Hargreaves Avenue
☎876-962-0388

Haughton's Pharmacy
18 West Park
☎ 876-962-2246

South Coast

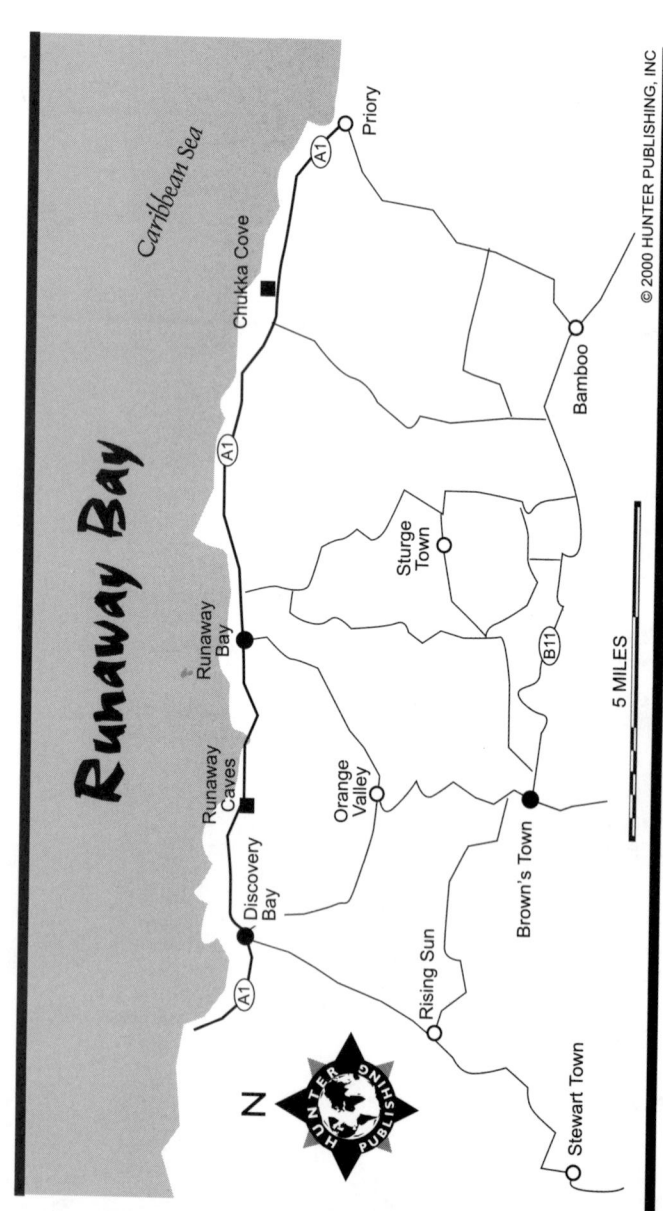

Runaway Bay

Caribbean Sea

Priory

Chukka Cove

Bamboo

A1

A1

Runaway Bay

Runaway Bay

Sturge Town

Runaway Caves

Orange Valley

B11

Discovery Bay

A1

Rising Sun

Brown's Town

5 MILES

N

Stewart Town

© 2000 HUNTER PUBLISHING, INC

Runaway Bay

Introduction

Runaway Bay is the smallest of the tourist destinations in Jamaica, a stop between Montego Bay and Ocho Rios. The area is actually a collection of several resorts and guests will find that day trips into either city are an easy task.

Best Places to Stay

Money Matters

Our price scale is designed to give you a ballpark figure for a typical stay during peak season. We've based these estimates on high season (December 15-April 15) for a standard room for two persons.

These prices do not take into account options, such as meal plans and dive packages.

Accommodations Price Scale

Prices are given in US dollars.

Deluxe. . . . . $300+
Expensive . . . . $200-$300
Moderate . . . . $100-$200
Inexpensive. . . . . Under $100

Resorts

BREEZES GOLF AND BEACH RESORT
North Coast Highway
☎ 876-973-2436, fax 876-973-2352
Reservations: ☎ 800/GO-SUPER
www.superclubs.com
Expensive to Deluxe (All-inclusive)

Breezes is a great choice for golfers and also offers a diversity of sports activities.

This property was one of our first stops in Jamaica, at the time a resort known as Jamaica-Jamaica. The property, still part of the SuperClubs chain, has seen many renovations and is still one of the most popular resorts on the island. Guests here enjoy use of a golf course and school right across the road, as well as tennis, horseback riding, windsurfing (with a Mistral school on property), and more. Rooms have a tropical decor and the grounds are always, as with all SuperClubs, immaculate.

FRANKLIN D. RESORT (FDR)
North Coast Highway
☎ 876-973-3067, fax 876-973-4600
Reservations: ☎ 800-654-1-FDR
www.fdrholidays.com
Expensive (All-inclusive)

This resort is a favorite with families. It offers a supervised children's program, but the resort also has a unique feature: Vacation Nannies. One nanny is assigned to every suite and tends to the children's needs; babysitting services in the evening are also available for a very low fee. The property is a big hit with the kids because they are offered everything a child could want: a kids' and teens' disco, an arts and crafts center (all the kids make leather necklace nametags for their first project), and more.

There's a full array of watersports as well and two peaceful bays that are calm enough for children's swimming.

GRAND LIDO BRACO VILLAGE RESORT
West of Runaway Bay on North Coast Highway
☎ 876-954-0000, fax 876-954-0020
Reservations: ☎ 800-GO-SUPER
www.superclubs.com
Expensive

New to the SuperClubs chain, this resort was built with the purpose of recreating a Jamaican village, and you'll find everyone from the peanut man offering fresh roasted goodies to the jerk cook to the woodcarver. The resort is built around a town square with cafés, art stores and a friendly feel. It's no substitute for getting out and experiencing a real Jamaican village, but for first-timers it can be educational and fun.

There's also a full array of all-inclusive diversions: tennis, soccer, golf, beaches and watersports.

Runaway Bay

Only adults are allowed at Grand Lido Braco Village.

Intimate Inns

RUNAWAY BAY HEART HOTEL
AND TRAINING INSTITUTE
☎ 876-973-2671, fax 876-973-2693
Reservations: ☎ 212-319-2100
Inexpensive

You will not find a more motivated staff than at the training hotel.

This hotel offers something a little bit different. It's a training institute operated by the government of Jamaica to teach young people skills of the hotel trade. There are just 20 rooms, each with air-conditioning, telephone, satellite TV and private bath.

The beach is a five-minute shuttle ride away; golf is available next door. The hotel contains the Cardiff Hall Restaurant for formal dining. The prices at this resort are a bargain.

Best Places to Eat

Money Matters

For dining, we've set up a price scale based on a three-course dinner including appetizer or soup, an entrée, dessert and coffee. Cocktails and wine are extra.

Dining Price Scale

Prices are per person in US dollars.

Expensive. . . . .$40+ per person
Moderate . . . . $25-$40
Inexpensive. . . . . Under $25

Recommended Restaurants

CARDIFF HALL RESTAURANT
Runaway Bay HEART Hotel
☎ 876-973-2671
Moderate

Local and international dishes fill the menu at this indoor restaurant, which serves seafood, steaks, salads and vintage wines. As a training institute, the restaurant offers classic European table service.

PIACERE
Grand Lido Braco
West of Runaway Bay on North Coast Highway
☎ 876-954-0000
All-inclusive

This elegant French restaurant is an excellent choice for a special evening. Reservations are required.

Entrées include creations such as sautéed chicken breast on soft polenta and fava beans; mille feuille of Angus beef tenderloin and wild mushroom ragout; lavender-glazed salmon with saffron whipped potatoes; smoked seafood spaghettini with boursin and caper sauce and

Reservations suggested on weekends at Cardiff Hall.

Runaway Bay

Wear your best clothes for dinner at Piacere.

sevruga caviar; and mustard and herb-crusted rack of lamb.

Sunup To Sundown

Beaches

Most of the action in Runaway Bay takes place on the town's beach: lounging on the sand, relaxing in the gentle surf, or swimming in the warm waters.

Nude & Topless Beaches

Grand Lido Braco has a clothing-optional beach, as does **Breezes Golf and Beach Resort**.

Golf

BRACO VILLAGE RESORT GOLF CLUB
West of Runaway Bay on North Coast Highway
☎ 876-954-0010

This nine-hole course and club includes a putting green and driving range. Par 28.

BREEZES GOLF AND BEACH RESORT
North Coast Highway
☎ 876-973-2561

This championship course sits across the street from the Breezes Resort and many of its guests use the excellent facilities. The course has hosted events such as the Heineken World Cup Western Zone Qualified and the Jamaica Open. The course includes a clubhouse, restaurant and pro shop. Par 72.

Runaway Bay A-Z ?

Emergency Phone Numbers

Ambulance 110
Police. 119
Fire 110

Information Sources

Internet Sites

JAMAICA TOURIST BOARD
www.jamaicatravel.com

This extensive website is an excellent resource for information on Jamaica attractions, accommodations, dining, special events and weather.

JAWEB YARD PAGE
www.pacificnet.net/~jaweb/index.html

This site promotes itself as "for Jamericans, Janadians, Janglish, and all JaPeople." It offers tips on visiting Jamaica, a listing of Jamaican businesses in the US and Canada, and even an alumni section on Jamaican high schools.

CARIBBEAN SUPERSITE
http://caribbeansupersite.com/jamaica

Accommodations, getting around, entertainment and food are covered here.

JAMAICA GLEANER
www.jamaica-gleaner.com

The *Gleaner* is the daily paper in Kingston and the best source of news on the island. An online version with the day's top stories is posted every weekday at noon on this site; other sections include a *Jamaica Yellow Pages* and tourist information.

Jamaican Travel Books

Baker, Christopher P. *Jamaica*. Lonely Planet Publications, 1996.

Fodor, *Pocket Jamaica*, Fodor's Travel Publication, 1998

Gordon, Sonia. *Insight Pocket Guide Jamaica*. Langenscheidt Publishers, 1998.

Henderson, James. *Jamaica and the Cayman Islands*. Cadogan Books, 1996.

Luntta, Karl. *Jamaica Handbook*. Moon Travel Handbooks, 1996.

Permenter, P. & Bigley, J. *Adventure Guide to Jamaica*. Hunter Publishing, 2000.

Permenter, P. & Bigley, J. *Jamaica: A Taste of the Island*. Hunter Publishing, 2000.

Porter, Darwin. *Frommer's Jamaica and Barbados*. IDG Books, 1998.

Smit, Hannie and Theo Smit. *Diving and Snorkeling Guide to Jamaica*. Lonely Planet Publications, 1996.

Smith, Martha K. *Jamaica: The Beach and Beyond*. Cuchipanda, 1997.

Thomas, Polly and Adam Vaitilingham. *Jamaica: The Rough Guide*. Rough Guides, 1997.

Wilson, Annie. *Essential Jamaica*. NTC Contemporary Publishing Co., 1996.

Zach, Paul. *Insight Guide Jamaica.* Langen-scheidt Publishers, 1996.

Appendix

Index

Index

Adventure Guides

This signature Hunter series targets travelers eager to really explore the destination, not just visit it. Extensively researched and offering the very latest information available, *Adventure Guides* are written by knowledgeable, experienced authors, often local residents.

Adventure Guides offer the best mix of conventional travel guide and high adventure book. They cover all the basics every traveler needs – where to stay and eat, sightseeing, transportation, climate, culural issues, geography, when to go and other practicalities – followed by the adventures. Whether your idea of "adventure" is parasailing, hiking, swimming, horseback riding, hang-gliding, skiing, beachcombing or rock climbing, these books have all the information you need. The best local outfitters are listed, along with contact information. Valuable tips from the authors will save you money, headaches and hassle.

Town and regional maps make navigation easy. Photos complement the lively text. All *Adventure Guides* are fully indexed.

Adventure Guides

Adventure Guide to Jamaica

Adventure Guide to the Leeward Islands

Adventure Guide to Maine

Adventure Guide to Massachusetts
& Western Connecticut

Adventure Guide to Michigan

Adventure Guide to Montana

Adventure Guide to Nevada

Adventure Guide to New Hampshire

Adventure Guide to Northern California

Adventure Guide to Northern Florida
& the Panhandle

Adventure Guide to Oklahoma

Adventure Guide to Orlando & Central Florida

Adventure Guide to the Pacific Northwest

Adventure Guide to Puerto Rico

Adventure Guide to the Sierra Nevada

Adventure Guide to Southeast Florida

Adventure Guide to Tampa Bay
& Florida's West Coast

Adventure Guide to Texas

Adventure Guide to Trinidad & Tobago

Adventure Guide to Vermont

Adventure Guide to Virginia

Adventure Guide to the Yucatán